Sowing Seeds of Justice

Sowing Seeds of Justice

Courage, Persistence and Faith
of African American Women in the Delta

Becky Williams
Author/Editor

Laurent Guerin
Photographer

Cypress
Knee
Press

Published by Cypress Knee Press
Little Rock, Arkansas

Cover Image: Gertrude Jackson, taken by Laurent Guerin.

Back Cover: DWAG members taking community assessment,
taken by Becky Williams

Photography by Laurent Guerin
except for the following:
Gould Black School, page 59
courtesy Wisconsin Historical Society, WHS-23661
Cotton bolls and field, pages 18 and 39 by Kat Robinson
Personal images from the community oral history project,
DWAG and DYAG, by Becky Williams

Design by Kat Robinson of Tonti Press, Little Rock

First published July 2020

Manufactured in the United States of America

ISBN 978-1-7347109-08

Library of Congress Control Number: 2020941027

To

These ten women

My family and friends
who supported
this work
during the twenty-one-year journey

In memory of Don Rothman,
my teacher, mentor and dear friend
who fought for justice
and taught me that I could,
in fact,
write.

"I don't know if that's good or not but when you make up your mind that you're going to do something, you just don't have any fear. And you know, the dangers and fear somehow or another just leaves. It's like the more you want to do, it motivates you to do more. That's what happened."

Gertrude Jackson, 2000

How it all goes

What this book is about

The last time I saw Gertrude

her small smile and quiet determination

disguised the fire within.

Even though she used a walker and proceeded slowly, there was no doubt in my mind this gentle woman still carried the strong spiritual presence I had first seen in Marvell, Arkansas the spring of 1998.

Gertrude, dressed in comfortable clothes and her red knit hat, moved straight ahead, in front of the information desk in the lobby of the nursing facility. She always walked like she had a mission to accomplish.

From organizing civil rights actions to driving children to Head Start to founding a community rights organization, Gertrude sowed seeds of justice all her life.

I knew this day that Gertrude no longer recognized me. She had no memory. She'd been like this for several months. Gertrude died in the fall of 2019.

Over the past 20 years however she had been telling me her story. Now it's time to share, along with the stories of nine other incredible African American women of the Arkansas Delta.

In these stories, each woman shared a life experience or crisis where she felt distressed, oppressed, hopeless or helpless; a second experience where she felt the competency and power to make decisions in her life and create more equity in her community; and what happened during her life that helped her change. Each woman chose the experiences from her life she wanted to share.

All lived in the two towns of Marvell and Gould, Arkansas when interviewed in 2003 and 2004. At different ages when interviewed, the women talked about different years in their lives. The earliest experiences shared took place in the 1950's. The most recent experiences shared took place in 2004.

The photographs present the stories of the women's lives through lenses of dignity and integrity. The color photos serve as a window into the daily activities of the individuals as well

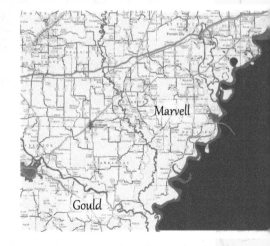

Marvell

Gould

as the characteristics of the region including customs and traditions, food, work, recreation and community.

As James Agee and Walker Evans stated in their work, *Let Us Now Praise Famous Men,* "The photographs are not illustrative. They, and the text are co-equal, mutually independent, and fully collaborative."

The first theme of the book is that these ten women remained in the Delta during their lives and that during this time from 1950 to 2004 great change occurred in the United States and the Delta that affected the women and how they lived.

During the fifty-four year period covered in the book, many African Americans left the rural Delta and moved to cities such as Little Rock, Chicago, Detroit, and Los Angeles looking for work and better living conditions. The ten women spotlighted in this book chose to stay in the Delta, go to school there, raise their children, join churches, and work. Often, they have lived in the same side of town, perhaps in the same house for many years. Some of their children moved to Little Rock or other states however they returned to the Delta for family reunions in the summer.

Many changes occurred during this time in the United States and in their two towns that affected their lifestyles. In the 1950's and 1960's most of the women grew up on farms in the country and often had no indoor plumbing, water or electricity. Their families produced much of their own food. A number of the women grew up in families with eight to twelve brothers and sisters. Their mothers worked on farms or worked in the homes of white residents as domestics. Few local healthcare services existed. Most attended segregated schools for part or all of their education. They advanced as far as a high school diploma.

As the years passed into the 1970's and 1980's circumstances began to change for the women. During this time each community or a town close by opened a health clinic offering family planning services which allowed the women to decide how many children they wanted. Women began attending college. Schools became integrated. Work changed to include a wider variety of jobs outside the home – janitor, prison guard, factory worker, nurse, and organization executive director.

The second theme is the challenges the women faced during their lives. Each woman selected the life struggles she wanted to discuss during the interviews. The issues ranged from the death of a five-week old son to domestic violence. Eight of the ten women shared experiences involving equality and social justice.

The third theme is how the women survived these struggles and became independent, contributing members of their communities. The women survived through courage, persistence and faith. They learned these from their mothers and grandmothers, their children, pastors, mentors, teachers, and friends. In addition, the women employed a toolbox of actions in their work for social justice. (*see Appendices 1-4, page 152-155*).

Over the years I have become close friends with most of the women in this book. We have spent time together and with their families. All the women have their feet planted solidly on the ground through their values of love and compassion.

They made choices in their lives and lived with the consequences. They chose to make their lives better and to help those around them. Their stories spotlight the women's values as well as practical tools for survival and for life. Please use their stories as you travel in your life journey. The women want you to do so.

Becky Williams
2020

Gertrude Jackson

The way we started, we were invited to this meeting,

my husband, me and other leaders in the community.

We had little children, must have been early 1960's. I guess we were considered some of the leading members of the community because we were the kind to go to a board meeting, or go to a PTA meeting, just kinda go forward.

It was inside Mr. Adams' house. Just a few people were there, about ten. Some sat in the living room, some were from out in the community. We went to the meeting to see what's going on. The only thing I knew was about the schools. Correcting the school system. The children I seen packed in the buses and packed in the classrooms and that's what really interested me.

The thing that sat in my mind most was there were lots of black people in this area at that time. Like we all had eight, ten, or twelve children. The school bus would come down and pick up the children. And what I remember mostly was that it was so packed, kinda like sardines.

The children was little and they would just go ahead and get on the bus. They'd go back, and if they put on the brakes on that bus you couldn't move forward or backwards because you're packed so tight. My daughter was talking one day and she said she got on the bus and they'd have to squeeze in so the driver could shut the door. They were packed on the steps all the way to the back.

At the children's school in Turner it was pitiful. Instead of the water flowing down hill, the way they graded it, the water went up hill. As a result, in the bathrooms and the hallways you'd always have stuff backing up - refuse, odors and everything. They kept sending people out there to fix it but they knew they couldn't fix it and they wouldn't go out and re-grade it.

The black school was actually a part of the Marvell School District. The school board, all white men, was responsible for the black school. It was a unified school district, just segregated schools. That was true all over the state where there were black communities.

At the meeting John Hamilton was one of the leaders. He brought them (Student Nonviolent Coordinating Committee workers - SNCC). In 1965, at that time they (SNCC workers) were just coming in from Helena, Arkansas. Howard Himmelbaum and another white man, and Merle Glasco, a black woman, all came from New York. They talked about New York and they was just interested in here.

When the civil rights workers first came in here some stayed in the community with John Hamilton. And the word got out that white people was gonna come down and go to John Hamilton and do something to him. And so the community got together about fifteen or twenty men, sit up all night around his house to watch, because he was back up off the road in a field and they could see if anything turned off, so they were there to protect him all night.

The next meeting was at my house the next week and there was about eighteen people. I felt like it was a natural step to have it at our house. Then a few more would come in, and they'd say, "What we gonna do now, we're gonna start having the meeting at the church." Then just a few key community people would go back and tell the others in their community. We would meet at our church, right by Highway 1, called Bridge Baptist, and then in Marvell at the Methodist Church.

Once we got over into the school integration and working in the school system and changing things around, it got very serious because there were some white people that weren't happy we were meeting. But they didn't know we were meeting at first. We had the meeting a good long time before they found out. We talked about keeping quiet. But we didn't just volunteer to talk to anybody.

I don't know if that's good or not but when you make up your mind that you're going to do something, you just don't have any fear. And you know the dangers and fear somehow or another just leaves. It's like the more you want to do, it's like to motivate you to do more. That's what happened.

And some how along they found out that we had been meeting a good while. One evening just before our meeting, just before dark, a truck pulled up over there at the highway right up from our house and shot the rifle and it went black around here.

I saw the truck, I was home, but you know, I really didn't know what had happened. And I told my husband someone come along and shot the wire before the electricity went out.

So we met that night for the meeting, with no lights. We still had some light in the church, so the white boys (SNCC workers) got a little nervous and said, "Let's move along tonight." And so we didn't stay long that night. The FBI came by and investigated and she said she didn't know anybody she could write up.

After the fellow shot the wire, we hired a person to stand shotgun at the church so wouldn't nobody come up. He was there every time we met down there. We knew him very well.

My husband and his brother were the head leaders in this area and they were farmers. We had on our farm a truck that he would haul over and then would go out and haul cotton pickers (machinery). One night they had taken his gas cap off and stuck some kind of rag in the gas tank.

One of my children had a ball in the house. I said, "Take that ball out of here." She went to put her ball outside and she started screaming that there was a fire. And my husband had gone to bed.

Evidently he had been looking for something all along because before she got that out, that man had his pants on and busted out of that chair. And so he found out what happened was the whole shed wasn't on fire, but the truck was burning up. After so long the gasoline was going to explode and so what he did he ran and got on that tractor and backed that tractor into the truck with the children screaming and hollering, "Come back Daddy, don't go out there Daddy." He hooked the tractor to the truck and hauled it across the field. And it burned up that night. So my children learned from that night.

And one other thing that happened to him. They were farming about ten or twelve miles from here, and they had been picking cotton. They left the cotton pickers out in the field and so my brother-in-law went to the field and he said he saw the little tractor tracks. To make a long story short, someone had been there and put what they said was sugar in the gas tank and they had just bought the cotton picker and it destroyed it.

Now my children, they say, "Mama ya'll just forgot, but there was a cross burning in our yard, they burned it in the ground." My children remember.

I just remember the truck set on fire, the tractors and the cotton picking bin torn up trying to discourage us. But also I remember people tried to keep us from getting loans. They went to the banker and talked to him to not let us have a loan to farm. We were still able to get a loan.

The way we found this out now, when the school got straight, the banker was talking to my husband and his brother and said, "Now you all kinda hold up now. You've got the school integrated and you done made a lot of enemies," and we did. He did tell us, "All your enemies are not white." He said, "We had people to come in and try to get me not to give ya'll a loan but I let them know that we were in a business and we couldn't stop giving loans." And that's what happened with that.

My husband came up with the idea of keeping the children out of school.

All that way home he said, "You know if I could get the people to take their children out of school, they would fix that back room."

The people that went to see (the conditions at the school) would drive around to the communities and tell more people about what we're going to do. So me and you go to Mt. Zion because we going to go to talk to people and that's what I call community homework, doing what needs to be done to get the people aware of what's going on. We went around and told everyone what was going on, planned to stay out of school on Monday.

My husband got up the next day and the people was just sitting around, like I say, no working going on. Started off with five or six and then they just spread through the community.

I snuck downtown Marvell and saw all these people crowded out on the street and in front of their stores and houses to protect themselves. They thought we were going to come protest and march in Marvell. Instead we kept the kids at home from school in Turner to protest.

It was in Turner at the school in 1966 where we decided to boycott. We called it "not going to school because of the conditions." Somehow, somebody got the Health Department involved. I mean Phillips County Health Department didn't do it. They would come down as if everything was all right and stuff like that and make us look bad. Finally the Health Department in Little Rock came and fixed the school. They fixed the school but we still had segregation.

I kept a letter from the secretary of the NAACP, a tall, slender man. We was deep in our boycotting the Marvell School District, it was working fine. The news came on the radio that the secretary of the NAACP says he thinks the people at Marvell are doing the wrong thing down there, boycotting. And so he brought that to a meeting one night and we said, we going to boycott. I wrote him a letter and he answered it. He said I didn't know nothing about Marvell, Arkansas. I didn't even know Marvell was having any problems. But we didn't fall for that one.

In 1968 we filed the lawsuit for desegregation.

I tell you what I thought this integration was about. I thought it was more a tradition; that's just the way things are. I didn't think they would rebel as much from the changes. But there was really lots of hatred there. Because like when they finally integrated and the children that went to the white school, there was a white lady that said the ones that go to this school will be sorry. We're going to really make it hard for them, which they did.

And what I couldn't understand, when I had my first baby that was so precious. Oh, a sweet baby. And they were tending these white folks. How could they let somebody they hate so bad come in and tend to their babies? I'd say, "That'd be bad touching my baby." I couldn't stand it. I thought what they mean when they say, "Go to the back door?" I just love my back door and the back steps. I tried not to take them really serious, it was just more a tradition.

My father owned our land. That's what one of the ladies told me. She said, "You all can work, you're on your own land." When the judge ordered the schools to integrate, this black lady was cleaning house for this man. One day she said she stepped up in the door, you know like she's going to work, and never knocked, says she stepped up in the door and this man and wife stopped her.

She said the wife was crying. Her husband say, "Before I let my child go to school with a nigger I'll send him overseas." She said, "He said that right in my face." And she said then he said, "Wait a minute, wait a minute, I didn't mean it like that, I didn't mean it like that. Because you know there is some good niggers."

She decided not to say a word because she said, "See I had a little black boy going out there to school. For that day I just took it easy until it worked where we could get off his place." That's what they did after a few years, they moved. But they were so serious, they were really serious.

I started work when I was 43 years old in about 1964. That was my first job. They were just starting the Mid-Delta Head Start in Marvell. They were looking for someone who had a station wagon and children. The man made a third trip down here looking for me, and my husband would always say no. Then at the last minute he gave up. My husband said, "How you going to find all those people?" A lady by the name of Fannie Lee Turner had gone ahead and gone around and found the students for Head Start.

It was my first time working out of the home. I felt good about it. And first, I started in this little raggedy station wagon that was leaking dust, and I thought those children sure had the nerve to get in the station wagon with me. I got so much per mile, 20 cents a mile and I would do 75 miles in the morning and 75 in the evening. I was transporting them to Marvell. I had to go all over this community to pick them up. Take in some, put them off and then go back out.

I went from transporting Head Start students to in the classroom teaching at Head Start. And after a few years, Home Start started, where you go to the homes. I was chosen to take ones that left the Head Start and went into the home and that was a great joy. We worked with the children; they were four and five years old.

You carry your games, your books, your reading stories, and you could bring a puzzle. I would have my monthly meeting with the parents and I could have it around 12:00 p.m. when the men come out of the fields. We'd have our refreshments and show films and things. And I really enjoyed that. Read the children stories, nursery rhymes.

Head Start was just taking so many and there were so many children out there. So these were the ones that couldn't go to Head Start. I was visiting a lot of different homes. So I saw what kind of issues they were concerned about. And what I could also do, like if there were three families kinda close, then they would all come to that one house. And then I had my baby and I had two children involved, and I would take them along with me. And that's what Home Start was.

From Home Start I was called in to be a director over services at Mid Delta. That's transportation to the doctor or whatever. It was where people come and get information, like a satellite center.

I was working there when Boys Girls Adults Community Development Center was born. I was just sitting at my desk one day doing my weekly report and the mailman just dropped in my mail and all it said was something for children. And that stayed there for about three months. I won't forget that. It just said "something for children."

I was sitting there at the desk at Mid Delta and we had just hired a new' teacher, an Agriculture teacher. He came in there one day and he says,

"Ms. Jackson, I see you got an extra room back there that's not doing anything." He said he was sure around here children don't have nowhere to go. "I would like to fix that room up so we could give these children somewhere to go." I got this thought, for the children, so that thought just kinda came to my mind. I sat there for about three minutes with it in my head.

And then an opportunity came and my first words were, "Boy, God must have sent you."

And we started from that moment. I had to call Mrs. Dobbs who was the director at Mid Delta and tell her what was on my mind. She said, "Well I tell you what you do, ya'll just come in and talk to me about it." We went in and talked to them and told them what we wanted to do.

Mid Delta was in the community and then they had a board that we would meet and see what we could do for the community. So she started, "I tell you what, O.B. Watkins is in that area where you live and he's on the board. I'll ask the board for $500 to help you get started." So we came back and met with all the people, the local parents and told them what Ms. Dobbs says.

So one man said, "Now she offered you $500, she'll probably give you $1,000." And that's where we started with that $1,000 and we got to fix the room and to show how the Lord was directing it, every evening he would bring ten or twelve boys down there to work on the room. I had to be there as director, to be in the building while they worked and then they finally got it finished.

And there was some little grant that he could get through the school, like $2,000 and so we went to the school system and asked them for that. When the board got to debating, one of the men said, "Well, go on and let them have it. The next couple of years you'll forget they ever started." This was the white school board. So they just let them have it. Couldn't hurt nothing no ways but it would help, at least it couldn't hurt.

We got started from that and the boys would come down and finally got that room fixed and we had the $2,000 and we bought two pool tables and he made a lot of games with the boys at the shop. And we moved in and to show you how we were blessed, there'd always be two or three men and they'd open twice a week for these boys to come down and play the games and on Saturdays. And everything was going smooth.

And then all of a sudden the entire roof had blown off this building, torn up. It leaked so bad that Mid Delta had to move out because the community had raised money over and over to put the top on and it'd last a few years and then it's gone again.

Mrs. Dobbs said, "Well we just going to have to move out. And what I'm going to do, I'm going to leave the roof covered up for six months to give you a chance to find somewhere to put your equipment." We couldn't find anything and we searched and searched.

So we started raising money ourselves. We would sell dinners on Saturdays and we had two or three ladies that could cook like you wouldn't believe. I thought it was amazing how we'd get on the phone and they'd buy the dinners. We had a fish fry where the men got together and they went somewhere and got the fish and they came together and cleaned the fish themselves because it was cheaper, and we sold fish and everything. We had dances or whatever to keep raising money for the new roof.

There was a roof but it rained all over. The only place that didn't leak was the two front offices. The other times during the rainy season you had to walk around there in your boots and we survived that. That same year I was concerned because I had experienced children that couldn't start school because they hadn't had their shots. So that was only my concern. Also I had experienced fifteen or twenty children out there that didn't get any pre-schooling because Mid Delta couldn't take but thirty and I don't know how many but a bunch of them couldn't get in to pre-school.

So after we had started I talked to the director and told her what I wanted and I said, "I would like for every child to start to school this fall with some pre-schooling." And so we organized and went into every home and taught them that summer. I remember about five or six ladies volunteered to go into the homes, and by me having gone through the community picking up children, I knew where everybody lived.

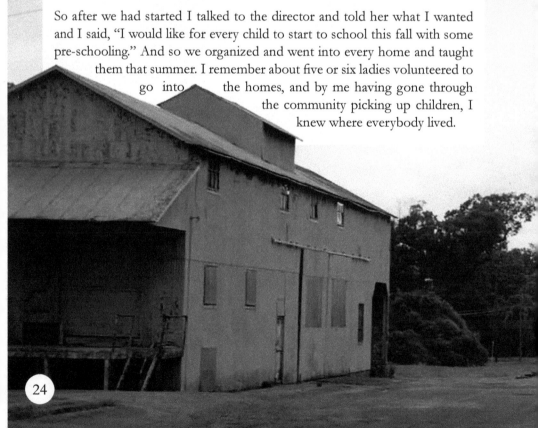

Each one of us took so many families and we went in all summer. We set up a little paint and easel on a tree and they would paint and just little things like that. And the next thing I wanted was for every child to have had their shots and the health department would come down to the center and that's where we'd take them and get their shots.

Also we formed a fifteen-member board and each board member agreed to pay $10 a month and that took care of the rent. There were fish fries and that took care of the utilities. And while we were in the middle of this, there was a man in Madison that was looking for communities that was doing something for children. And we got in touch with him and that's the first money we got.

We'd always say we were started in 1978, and named it the Boys, Girls, Adult Community Development Center. The young man that was one of the founders named it. He said, "What we gonna name it? Well, we are the adults, and we're here for the children and that's too much to say." But we went on and named it that.

When I look at it and I say I know the Lord put this on my mind. I think we was preparing for a time like this, when it's done gone so bad that we really need it, now much more so than when I look back.

Mostly I could see we needed the children to prepare to go to school with some education like pre-schooling, and with the integration, they had that then to get into school. And it seemed at that point was our biggest problem.

Then so much come on now, like we have the little ball games that they have. It has drawn a lot of little boys and brought them out of the streets and like the men are working so diligently with them and

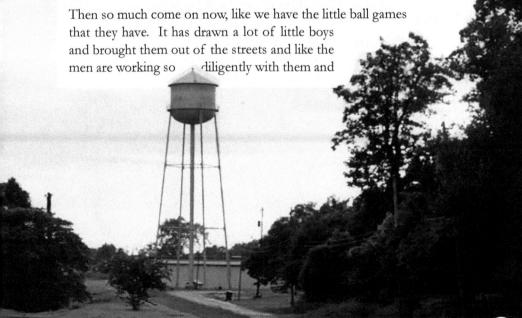

we had a great team last year. So I could see it coming on because one thing, we've always wanted men. So we got the men involved now and I'm looking forward to more men.

I tell you another reason. When we was here thirty years ago, you didn't see as many babies having babies. And now we have this program they called The Young Moms. We have that going and that's how Ernestine helps them. Maybe some we can't help but then there's a lot we do help. I think the one thing I've really learned after all this, if you working with twenty people and you save one of them, you've done a great thing if you can just save some of them.

Now I couldn't say that every-thing happened like this. To me this was just a special thing and that's why I believe in it so. To me it was special from Jesus. Just something is coming and you all need to be prepared for it. Then things just dropped down, all these drugs, all this killings and we need to try to do something. Even though we don't know exactly what to do, I know some of the things we are doing is reaching a lot of the children.

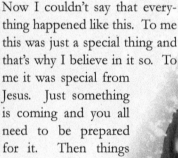
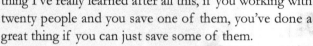

Jean Davis

When I was growing up
my family did not own anything, we'd sharecrop.

My daddy had about fifteen or twenty acres. I picked cotton between thirteen and twenty years of age. I was kinda late starting because I was always the house girl for my parents. They had to work out in the fields. My mother and daddy liked a big family, had ten children, so as the oldest girl I was always home with the babies, starting the cooking, taking care of the house.

I lived outside Keo, Arkansas in a rural area on the farm. We lived in what you called a shotgun house. It was just a straight wood house with about three rooms. We had no electricity until I was about seven or eight and no running water inside. We used kerosene lamps and cooked on a wood stove. Everybody raised a garden and we pretty much ate all the vegetables. We raised hogs, which was your pork meat, we raised the cows, which was your beef meat, and we raised chicken, turkeys, geese, ducks, and guineas. All the fowl that you used, you raised it. There were five or six other families on the same farm sharecropping. We played with those kids.

I was born in my great grandmother's house in 1936 when my mom went to North Little Rock and lived with her grandmother for a couple of years. My great grandmother was tall and kinda on the heavy side and was mixed with Indian. She had long salt and pepper hair and she always wore it busted down the middle in two braids. I loved to comb her hair. We'd visit often.

My mother was a kind-hearted person and she cared about people. She did all she could for us. Doesn't seem like it was much, but it was all she could do, and I appreciate her for that. She had a lot of children and she had one miscarriage and then she had one child die between my oldest brother and me. She had her children real, real, fast. And she worked a lot. She sewed a lot for us, and she was a real good cook. She canned a lot. So she did everything she could for us.

My dad was a sharecropper. He was a hardworking man, also a gambler and a drinker. Daddy worked hard when he wasn't drinking. He didn't drink until he made a little money to buy the stuff to make beer with because he was a bootlegger. He had a crock and churn, what you churn milk and butter in and he made beer in that type of stuff. People bought beer back then, but daddy made it.

He would chop cotton, pick cotton, he and mama would can foods, make keels to put potatoes in for the winter. But as soon as we picked the cotton and if we got out of debt, daddy would go gambling and lose the money. We never really prospered anything but we never went hungry either.

I never saw him hit mom but when he would come off his drinking or gambling spree, that's when the abuse would come in. One particular time will stay with me all of my life. I was a little girl, I can't imagine what age I was. They was gambling back in the back room and I didn't know it. As children we didn't know what was going on. My mama didn't want this to happen but my daddy did it anyway. He made mama come back up in the sitting room or the children's room and he sat with the gun cross his lap to make her stay up there and I guess to keep her from interfering with what was going on back there. It was scary. I will never forget that.

One particular time, daddy and mama had gotten into it verbally. I guess my brother who was two years older than me was gonna intervene. Seems like my brother went in and said something to him and my daddy told him to get out. Then I stepped in and he told me if I didn't like it, I could get out too. We were all the oldest ones. We wanted to go but didn't have anywhere to go so we had to stay there and take whatever he said to mama. Mama was on the verge of leaving him anyway, but he didn't know it. Mama just kinda shooed us off, saying, "Take it easy."

But there's something I haven't told you.

Our house was just a straight wood house with about three rooms. The big children slept in a room, mom and dad slept in the sitting room along with the smaller children. I think there were two of us sleeping in one bed, me and my nine year-old sister. There might have been other people in the bed, maybe three of us. The boys were in another bed in the same room. I was the oldest girl at home.

One night Daddy thought everybody was asleep and came into our room. I must have been about thirteen or fourteen. It was too dark to really see him but you know your family members. Everybody was asleep, including me but he woke me up when he said, "Scoot over." He was trying to get in the bed with us. But I couldn't scoot over. It just wasn't room to move over with three people in the bed. I didn't say anything. He said he was trying to show me something for my own good and I didn't know what daddy could be showing me for my own good in bed.

Before he tried to get in bed with me the first time, I got along with him okay. Just like regular daughter and father. I was really surprised when he came that night. I got a funny fear, I knew it wasn't right. But I didn't specifically know what he was trying to do and I didn't know what to do.

> I didn't want to scream 'cause that was daddy but I felt
> daddy didn't have no business being there
> and I just laid there.

He hadn't done this before, why would he want me to scoot over and get in the bed to show me something?

I guess he sensed I couldn't move over without waking up the others, and he should have known that before he come in there. He left but I guess a week passed, he came back again.

Like I said, I was thirteen or fourteen years old. I wasn't really dumb to the fact but then again, I was dumb to the fact. I never experienced nothing like that. Me and my girlfriends had begun to talk about little personal things and it was just a funny feeling.

When he'd come in there it was like a dream to me. Then it came to me: I'm not dreaming. My daddy is really coming in this room. I was scared because it happened about four times, whole total. I don't think my dad would have been drinking when he came in our room at night. He knew what he was doing. He said he was trying to teach me what to do.

I thought it was strange and finally I talked to my sister, who was nine, about it, the one next to me in bed. She said, "You know I thought I heard somebody in the room but I thought I was dreaming too." And I said, "The next time he do that I'm gonna wake you up." So I did and it kinda scared him off and he tried to end up with us but he realized both of us knew what was going on. I was afraid he would come back but he didn't. I'm glad he didn't 'cause I don't know what might have taken place then. Maybe he sense that he had gone too far.

My sister and I kinda like teamed up and that's when we went to my mother. She just went to praying. I do remember her saying, "I've got to go, we've got to go." So, I did not know what was going on but then later on I guessed she had contacted her brother.

I'm glad my mama understood us and reacted to us because if we'd stayed there I don't know what might have happened. That's one of the reasons that my mother kept leaving my father. She realized she had to do something about that and I'm glad she did. I was glad we were leaving.

That was just a dark age in my life.

My mother and us, the children, we chopped cotton and saved our money and her brother lived in Holly Grove and she contacted him and he sent her some money. So we was kind of stashing things back and getting things prepared. It took about six months. When the time was right, then we was able to leave.

At different times of day he would be away from home and on this particular day he had gone fishing. Daddy went one way going fishing and we got our little packs and went the other way to Keo to catch the Greyhound bus. And we only had what we could carry on our backs and the little children because

Jean Davis

all of them couldn't walk as far as we had to go. At this particular time I believe there was ten of us children and I was about fourteen. It was about 11 a.m. in the morning and it was daylight.

I don't remember what was in the bag but we each had a bag, like a pillow-case. We had clothing. My mother had a friend and she stashed a quilt. My mother pieced beautiful quilts and lots of household stuff like quilts and little spreads and sheets and she didn't want daddy to destroy these because he would get angry because she left. She stashed it down at her friend's house and it was part of the separation. We just carried what we could.

We had to walk about three or four miles to the bus and it was summer and so hot! I had one brother that was two years older than me, he was watching out for Daddy. Then when we got a certain distance we knew he wasn't come back. Usually when he went fishing he stayed for a long time so we was counting on that.

We caught the bus to Holly Grove and then switched from Greyhound to what you called Brocater Bus and then the Brocater come right by my uncle's house so we was able to get off the bus  right in my uncle's yard. He was there to meet us. We was glad to see him and glad that he did what he did for us and he had a lot of children too. My mama had ten, I think at this time, uncle must have had about eight or ten himself. There was just a four-room house and there was all the children and three adults, but we made it. We made it.

We enjoyed each other.

My daddy was kinda tight on us. Maybe we weren't old enough to go and we really didn't have anywhere we could go either. At my uncle's we was able to walk about two miles to town and do little things on Saturday nights. We was able to walk to school, to ball games, and little socials and stuff at school so we was able to participate in that. Whereas down where we live in Keo we was not able to do that so it was quite a bit more fun for us.

My uncle and my mother was share cropping. He cared for us all the way, I could always go to my uncle. We always felt like we had enough to eat. I guess a lot of that was the gardening, you could can the foods. In the summer we raised a garden and we canned, peas, corn, just whatever you get out of the garden. The most fun time we ate out of the garden and from the fruit trees.

We raised hogs, chickens for us. You didn't put the chickens up; you'd just go out in the yard and get them. Well, you'd kill the hog and salt the pork down so it would carry through the winter.

Then in the fall the farmers would plow their crops and then you'd get to work out some, gather crops. You paid off your debt then you had money left over most of the time where you could buy food to get you through the winter. My mother and father bought flour by the barrel, one hundred pound barrel. Meal, sugar and stuff by the barrel. Of course we had five gallon cans for baking – you'd have Wesson oil and peanut oil and we had what you called lard.

In March when you was running out of food you got furnish. I think we only got that for maybe three or four months. It means you could go to the commissary store. They would give you coupons and you could go there and get whatever the coupons would buy, maybe about thirty dollars a month worth. You could go there and take up this much goods. You'd gather the food and you'd take it back home. And that's how we made it from March until farming work start.

While working at a cafe in 1960 I met my husband and we dated and married within three months. I was twenty-three years old. I moved to Marvell and my next job I worked private home work. I washed and ironed clothes and cleaned houses. From there I went to a nursing home. I worked there for five years as a cook.

Then I went to the sewing factory in 1969. When I was young I would go visit my great grandmother. She had this sewing machine that was not electric, what you called a pearl machine. She'd sit me up in her lap and let me pull on a string or something and I enjoyed that, I guess because my great grandmother was doing it.

The sewing factory was in West Helena on the Mississippi River about ten miles from Marvell. The plant opened in about 1954. It was an old, ragged building with raw beams, machines plugged up overhead. Inside it sounded like heavy machines running, like rain coming down. The smell depended on what kind of dye was used in the materials. They used formaldehyde and some people suffered from that but it had no effect on me. Some people wore masks for the lint, there was a lot of lint.

My aunt went to the unemployment office for a test to work at the factory. I took her there and the lady giving the test said, "Well you're the only one setting up in here so why don't you take the test for the hell of it." I didn't have anything to lose so I said okay. I took the test and it was the funniest thing that I had ever seen.

I sat down to take the test to work there. When I put my foot on the pedal, the machine jumped, it scared me to death almost. The lady laughed at me. I asked if I could try it again, I had never did nothing like that in my life. She said yes. I tried it again and I passed the test and I worked there for twenty-nine years.

When I first started working at the factory there were about fifty black people.

Women and a few men worked there. You had to be at least eighteen years old. We made ladies sport jackets, hundreds and hundreds of them. I learned to operate four feet long, heavy-duty machines. The machines were sectioned off in squares with an aisle going down in between. One section would maybe do one side of the jacket and another section would do the other side. Within that section you've got your sleeve setter, pocket setter, side seamer, rigging, pressers, inspectors, whatever it takes to make that jacket. Then it goes on down to final press and inspection. A lotta times it would come back for repairs.

My work was piece work. I was guaranteed $3.35 an hour, twenty cents above minimum wage. I could make more than that though. I could make maybe as high as $5.00 an hour, depending on how many minutes I was making the run of the day.

The first day I worked there I felt strange, lost, didn't know what to do or expect but I survived. I didn't plan to work there long but as the years went by, I enjoyed it.

It was kinda gradual that I got into this work with the union. As soon as I started to work the girl I was driving with she was already working there. She introduced me to going to the union meetings and I slowly got involved, enjoyed it. I'd been going about two to three months and I began to learn about the union and signed a card to join and began to pay union dues. We had meetings once a month.

I had never been into anything like that until I started working down there. I was affiliated with the union, ILGW (International Ladies Garment Worker's Union), which is connected with the AFL-CIO. It must have started around 1959. When I worked in the union it was blacks and whites together in 1969. It was pretty accepted to have this organization in Arkansas with blacks and whites together.

People could join if they wanted to, but they didn't have to. There was no pressure on them one way or the other. When they filled out an application for work, they supposedly had to be issued a little card that they filled out as to whether they wanted to join or not. Some joined and some didn't. The majority of them would join. I had to find those that would stay, like I did. A lot of people just come and go, so you learn who they are as you go. Now the union is called Unite Now.

First I became a line stewardess and I would take care of the complaints on the part of the employees in my section. I didn't know these people before I started working there. Part of my job would be to stay in really good communication with the other workers on my part of the line by being observant. Maybe a worker was sewing over bad work. I needed to know this so I could report it to the chairperson who was over the whole plant. She took care of all the grievances as they came into her.

I also became an assistant chairperson. When the actual chairperson was absent, I had to take charge and see to the grievances. I would go and meet with management and the supervisor. Sometimes the person with the grievance would meet with us. This would help so we could really understand what he or she was talking about. We tried to resolve it the best we could. Sometimes we had to negotiate or compromise. Some of them didn't get resolved, but most of the time we got them resolved. We talked until the employee and employer would be halfway satisfied.

One day there was this lady, her name was Jean Day and she sewed side seams and shoulder joining. Jean was having a problem with her work and her machine needed some minor adjustment in order for her to do her job well. She hollered out "Section" and wanted the manager to come over into the section and just take a look.

The manager was already upset because he had just dealt with another person. He exploded on Jean and took her to the office and issued her a yellow slip. They would give yellow slips and when you got three of them within a year, then you would be fired. I was called in, they were yelling at each other. His name was Bobby and I had to get between them cause they were just yelling and yelling. It was going to lead to her getting fired. He exploded on her for no reason at all. I just talked to them. "Bobby, you hush, Jean, you hush." Jean started, "Well, he…" I said, "Jean you listen to Bobby." Then Bobby started, "Well Jean…" I said, "Bobby, listen to Jean. She has a right to talk and you have a right to talk. So let's just listen to each other like adults." So little by little, I calmed them down. Jean didn't get fired, she was one of the best workers there so everything worked out okay.

You had to be a union member for at least two years before you could hold an office. The first office I held was delegate at large and that's where the traveling came in. I went to different conventions, meeting out of town. The first time I really went on a trip was to Little Rock because we were affiliated with the AFL-CIO with Bill Becker. We would go to meetings in Little Rock, Hot Springs up in their area. We supported different labor movements, and at the meetings they would inform us about that. Bill Clinton was Governor and running for President, we supported him. They would inform us about him and Blanche Lambert in her run for Senator of Arkansas. We were there to observe and bring back to our local workers information that was provided.

It felt good to go to these meetings. I like to travel. I never had the opportunity when I was growing up and in my early adult life, I was afraid to because I had not experienced it. But the older I got, the more I liked to travel and sightsee. I went to Little Rock, Hot Springs, Columbus and St. Louis, Missouri, Washington, D.C., Miami, Florida, even went on a four-hour cruise.

Next I was elected to vice president of the local labor board. It was just like the school board where you go and discuss things and bring it back to the local union. Our union number was 525 and was made up of members within the local at West Helena. Then I was elected to president of the local because I attended the local meetings and I didn't miss a lot from work.

I got to go to Washington D.C. on Solidarity Day, Labor Day, September 1981. The membership elected me as a delegate to represent them. Representatives from other unions in different parts of Arkansas also traveled to the Solidarity Day.

On that day there were so many people that traveled from different parts of the country to Washington. We met people from all over like Canada and New Mexico. All the unions were there – ILGW, the steel workers and others, and they were identified somehow with their union. Some had the same colored t-shirts. We all had on heavy capped tee shirts. Mine was red and had our local number on it 'cause we were combined with other locals within the region. We all were ILGW.

By the Washington Monument, there was standing room only. One of our reps had already picked our spot overnight so he knew exactly where to drop us off by the Washington Monument.

I never saw that many people in my life at one place. You could hardly walk through 'em. It was extremely hot that day for Washington D.C. and they were spraying people down with fire hoses. Fire trucks were in different areas spraying them down for coolness. We just kinda walked around a little bit, not too far, you couldn't get far on the account of people, they were like hair on a dog's back.

The day was to celebrate Solidarity. To me that means that people can work together, understanding each other. When Jesse Jackson out of Chicago spoke, there were so many people, I could not see him, but I did hear him. I saw people coming from every direction there in the park. I just couldn't have imagined this; it was so pretty to me. It made me wonder if this is what heaven would look like.

I guess I've had to endure quite a bit, so I guess that made me strong.

Because I have had to just step up and be, I guess, a role model for my sister and brothers. Sometimes it seemed like it didn't help any. But then I've always, my brother and I, we've always had to be the ones to help out.

My education from life experience comes through working at the sewing factory. The important lessons about life and about working with people that I learned through being part of a union include how to get along with people better. I learned that everybody's not the same, and just because I think this way and you think another way, sometimes in the final face of it, we both would be right. You just come to the conclusion from a different angle.

I need to listen to you to see where you are coming from, and you need to listen to me to see where I am coming from. That way we can get an understanding. We end up agreeing most of the time on the same thing. I've used that in other parts of my life.

Also we used to go see my great grandmother a lot. And we enjoyed going up there to see her. She raised my mother. So some of my strength came from my great grandmother.

Several other women have helped me and were important in developing my beliefs and values. Annie Garner was a real old lady. She was very little and short and she liked to talk a lot. And she liked to go shopping and sightseeing. I'd put her in the car with me and take her to Helena. We'd look at the Christmas lights or whatever, depending what time of the year it was. She would keep tabs on me and sometimes I'd just go down there and sit on the porch and sometimes my family wouldn't be at home and I'd just go down there and curl up in her bed and go to sleep. She shared her life experiences. I learned from her how to treat people, how to be who you are. How to try to get along with everybody.

Also I was drawn to Miss Beatrice Shelby, my mother-in-law, from the time that I came to Marvell until she passed, which was the biggest part of my life. She was a Christian lady and was president of the usher board at her church. She went to church a lot. I loved to hear her sing. She would tell me how to get along with people. Annie Garner and Beatrice Shelby would tell me some of the things that they went through in life. They let me know that some things that happen is just the way life goes. It's not always good, and it's not always bad. But life is just life.

My daddy was a heavy drinker, and I always told myself if I ever got married, I would not marry a drunkard. It taught me something. I was twenty-three years old before I got married because I just could not go through what my mother went through. So I could handle myself pretty good.

I've seen different people I wanted to be like but not exactly like them but you know it's just some things you want to be like. To me there's no two people in the world exactly alike. I think everybody ought to be like their own person and I try to tell my grandchildren that too, just be you.

Regardless to what nobody else do, you just be you.

45

Essie Cableton

Being a black woman and living in the Delta during the 1940's through the 1960's where income and resources were limited, there were numerous times I experienced oppression. Try as you may, it seems that someone or something tries to keep you down. However, the most devastating time that I can remember occurred on January 5, 1991 when I was employed as a correctional officer at the Arkansas Department of Corrections Women's Unit.

I was about fifty years old and out of loyalty to my job, trying to keep my job, and with raising a family, needing my job,

I went to work sick.

I followed the policy of letting the supervisor know so she would be considerate if you were caught in a position where you were labeled as being asleep. This particular morning about an hour and fifteen minutes before getting off work, I was sitting with my head down. My supervisor said that I was asleep and I was terminated.

That was a very, very oppressive time. I got high blood pressure from that experience, never had a problem with my blood before. I felt like I should have been exonerated because of my loyalty even though the policy said if you are caught asleep, it's an automatic termination. The fact is, I went to work sick and that should have been considered.

It took almost four years to get my job back.

I started to work at the women's unit September of 1986 as a security officer. I supervised and monitored the inmates' movements and activities within the prison. I had no experience; I started at a beginner's level. We had to go to a six-week training process before we were permitted to go on duty. I got the job through a very good friend of mine, Vera Hampton. I had been working as a sewing machine operator in a factory in McGehee, Arkansas. Vera called me on Tuesday and asked if I wanted to work at the women's unit in security. "Oh, yes," I said. She said, "Be here Thursday morning for an interview." I went, interviewed, and was hired.

When I worked at the women's unit we had a population of about 280. Women were in prison for drug offences, bribery, thievery, shoplifting and some petty things. Some were there for murder, maybe killing their husbands or some member of the family. I worked eleven at night to seven in the morning. The women had to get up at 4:30 a.m. for work detail; some went to the laundry, different job activities. I worked with one living unit of thirty or forty women. My working conditions were good. I enjoyed working there. It was a good job, the women behaved and I developed a connection with them like being my children. The facility was in good condition. I had health insurance and retirement. Up until that time my job had gone pretty well.

The inmates in the prison called me "Granny." I feel they looked up to me and substituted me for their grandmother that they had at home. Most of them talked about, "If I had listened to what my grandmother told me, I wouldn't be in here."

The day before, I had the flu. I was really sick. I came to St. Elizabeth's Health Center here in Gould and the doctor was not in. All weekend I went to work. On that day I went to work at 11 p.m. I couldn't talk and I had to whisper. I was working in PBX, the Control Center, where everybody that comes in to the prison has to sign in and the units call in their counts of numbers of prisoners.

I was functioning pretty good but still I was sick. Everyone knew I was but I was still trying to make it because we're always short. My girlfriend told me prior to stop by her house. I would go early, stop by her house and go to sleep, then go to work. She said, "You don't need to go tonight, you're not feeling good." I told her I'd probably be able to make it. "If I stay at home, I'm not going to feel any better." I told my supervisor I was sick, that was the policy, and she said, "Okay." I didn't document anything.

That morning after all the movements had been completed, almost time to go home, I was sitting in a position not feeling really well at all, she walked up to the window and said, "Mrs. Cableton, you are asleep." I said, "No ma'am, I'm sick. I've got another

one of those dizzy spells and I've been feeling really bad." She said, "I relieve you of your duties." Just like that and I couldn't say anything else. She called the major who agreed with her and I was fired.

I felt like it couldn't be real, are they really doing this? They know that I am always at work; I don't miss unless it's scheduled. I don't call in sick so if I say I'm sick, they should have taken that into consideration. I brought them documentation showing I had come to the doctor but was unable to see him. It didn't do any good. I was just gone and I didn't know what to do about it. I didn't know how to feel about it. It was just something I had to live through which was not easy.

The termination wasn't so devastating. It was the fact that there was no consideration for my loyalty, commitment, dedication. I had gone to work in snow waist-deep where I could've stayed at home. When the weather started getting bad, I would pack a bag and stay over at the unit three or four days trying to be loyal. To have my credibility with my job tossed out of the window in a matter of minutes was just a devastating situation.

I was about fifty years old and I financially supported myself, two daughters and three grandchildren. I told my family I didn't have a job and I could not provide them with the essential things that I'd been giving them. Through the help and grace of God, we would make it. They supported me because they knew it was not my fault.

I filed an appeal and the Director of the Prison System upheld the decision that I be terminated. I then went to the second phase of the appeals process with an attorney. They recommended that I be rehired, but it took over three years for me to get my job back.

I kept putting in applications and being denied. My girlfriend told me the warden said before I would come back into Corrections, it had to be through a higher power.

> ## So I started praying
> ### and that is what I believe got me my job back

I prayed that I would meet the warden, Ms. Wallace, face to face. One day before the fourth of July a girlfriend and I went to Pine Bluff to find a goat to roast. Coming back, Harvest Foods grocery had posted a sign in the window, "ribs on sale." I said, "Let's stop by here and see what they look like." I entered the store and went to the dairy area where a woman was standing. I said, "That looks like Ms. Wallace; no it can't be." I had never before, nor since, seen her in a grocery store. I walked past her and she said, "How are you doing, Ms. Cableton?" I said, "Haven't I been punished enough?" She said, "Go fill out your application."

I did that and she released me to be hired by another prison unit in Dermott, Arkansas. After much energy and work I was finally hired by the Dermott Unit in 1994. I know that it was no power of my own because as an individual, I am powerless. It's the power of Him who strengthens me that I am able to handle any situation. Every day I go to work now, I have a little motto that I say, "There's nothing that me and God can't handle."

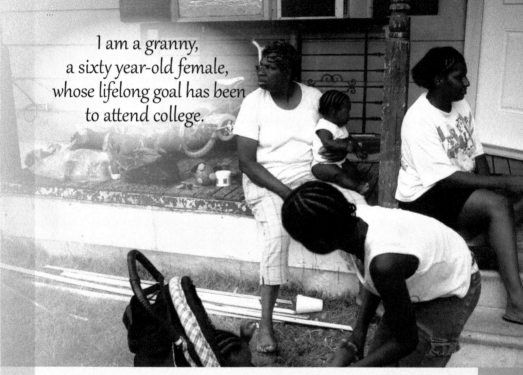

I am a granny, a sixty year-old female, whose lifelong goal has been to attend college.

For as long as I can remember, I have had a desire to go to college, if only for one day. Upon graduating high school with two children, I went to work in a sewing factory with the intent of earning enough money to fulfill my goal. No one had exposed us to loans, grants, and other benefits that are now available for obtaining a college education. After twenty years or more working in factories, no college. Not even close because there just wasn't enough money.

I have accomplished many things in my life and been many places, but none of them filled the void to go to college. One night I was telling my shift captain that I was planning to retire in the next two years because I would be sixty-two. He said, "Sage, do you know that when you turn sixty, you can attend any college you want to and the government will pay for it?" "Hey!" I thought. "Here's my chance of a lifetime!" I told him I would check into it.

So I went up to Southeast Arkansas Community College in Pine Bluff. When I completed my application, the man asked how I was going to pay for this and I asked, "Is there a program called Age Exempt?" He said, "That's all you need; are you sixty years old?" I said, "Yes I am." He said, "That's all you need; now you are enrolled in SEARK College!"

On August 20, 2001, I enrolled as a freshman at SEARK. Now "Look at Granny!" I am sixty years old and in college for the very first time. I have a 3.78 grade point average and hope to graduate in May. The moral of the story is, "Don't give up; you're never too old to accomplish your goals if you are determined. You may have a lot of setbacks in life, obstacles, hills, and problems, but if you are determined it will work out for you."

I'll be sixty-three when I graduate with an associate degree in Criminal Justice. I have not decided yet if I'm going to transfer to the University of Arkansas at Pine Bluff to get a Bachelor's degree. I've always said if I could just go to college one day I'd accomplished a milestone. The Lord made it possible and I've been there now for two years. I'm getting older now and I don't know if I want to puzzle my brain. But my daughter who is also in college says I'm going to transfer.

At this point I'm really happy with the accomplishment and the opportunity to fulfill this dream.

To help me get through the struggle, friends were supportive – they would encourage me to not give up, you're going to find something. After I was terminated, I knew that I had to move forward, I couldn't just quit and I always felt that I would go back. I was persistent and knew I would eventually get the job back. That mental attitude was something to hold on to and look forward to. I had this feeling, "Why am I going through this, what have I done to deserve this?" I felt like I was going through a conditioning period so I didn't feel any anger. I just felt like I had to get myself together.

I would tell someone going through the struggle, don't give up. Don't let anybody cause you to hold your head down. Pull yourself together. Keep your mind focused and just go on.

Don't let nobody steal your joy.

Don't let anybody cause you to doubt yourself because if you've got the will power, determination and strength, you can come through it. If you mope around and give up and feel sorrow for yourself then you can't make it. You have to put God first and follow his lead.

I tell people at work every day, you can't stop people from doing things to you. If you stand for right, stand for what you believe in and hold firm to that then you can overcome. It'll work out for you.

As long as I stay active and healthy as I am I will continue to do something and I just want to be an inspiration to others that feel like maybe it's too late or too old or I can't. If you got will power and determination, it's never too late.

Ecclesiastes 3:1 reads, "To everything there is a season, and a time to every purpose under heaven." I thank God that my time finally came.

Clora T. Green

I was born here in Gould, out there in the country on a farm. There was seven of us, four girls and three boys, I'm in the middle. We had two horses, a pig and a couple of chickens, two dogs, a cow and a calf. We chopped cotton and beans and we raised sweet potatoes and okra, greens and watermelons, squash. Our house was surrounded by pecan trees. We had three pear trees out across the field. We ate mostly out of the garden. We were fed, clothed and had a place to live and went to church on Sundays.

Mom would cook rice, beans and corn bread, black-eyed peas and okra, fry bologna on weekdays. On Sundays she would fry chicken, put some gravy to it and we'd still eat rice. She cooked her own bread, biscuits.

We'd go to Dumas, to the dollar store, Wolf Brothers and Sterlings - that I can remember, our doctor was in Star City. We went to my sister's house in Pine Bluff once or twice a year and my daddy had a sister that stayed in Dewitt, we went there two or three times a year. We didn't do too much traveling.

We had our own land. The farm belonged to my mother's folks and her daddy had the house built. He was a sharecropper. They sectioned the land off and this sister got this, and this sister got that part. My mother was the youngest of eight children and she got the section of the land with the house. My baby sister lives in the house now.

I rode the bus to Gould Elementary School. We were all together and we didn't have to change rooms. Just one teacher until we got to seventh grade then we change classes and had different teachers.

My parents said, "Stay in school so you won't have to be chopping cotton all your life."

I think mom went to eighth grade. I don't know how far my dad did. My mom knew how to read and write, my dad could write, I don't know if he could read or not.

With us staying
out in the country, we didn't come to town
very much so I liked going to school, just to be at school and away
from around the house, except when it rained because we had to walk from
the house to the highway in the rain.

Schools were integrated in seventh grade. In high school black and white students were together and we didn't have no problems. I didn't have no problems with 'em, 'cause see when we go to class the white kids would sit over there and we would sit over there but we would communicate with them, we just didn't sit together. I didn't know any of the white kids before we started going to school together.

When I became a teenager, I didn't go to many school activities, I lived with my parents in the country and three other siblings but we didn't worry about it. I didn't stay at home too long. I graduated in May of 1973 and got married in September of 1973.

Mrs. Freeman, my first grade teacher in my one room schoolhouse, was important. She made sure we learned. If we didn't, she'd peck us on our hand when we made a mistake and she had told us. She had good confidence in us. She would give us encouragement that we could do it if we tried. Later I had the confidence in myself that I could do it. Also I would say Mrs. Medlock, my high school English teacher. She would tell us that we'll learn one day, we'll be grown and faced with some situations. If we try we'd be successful, turn out all right.

I guess she was talking about faced with different kinds of people, different personalities. At that time I wasn't thinking about it either. But you think back to what older folks told you, "Just keep on living, you'll see things you never seen before." I liked all the subjects except science, doing insects and bugs, ugh….

My future husband and me grew up together. He stayed out there in the country, they were our neighbors. I'd been knowing him since I was about nine years old. We were girlfriend and boyfriend for a long time.

We decided to get married in September in 1973. He was in the Army and I moved in town with his mama until he got out of the Army in 1976. He was stationed at Fort Hood Texas, then Fort Polk, Oklahoma. He stayed six months in Germany. I didn't go. I'd be in touch with him by telephone and wrote letters. But he'd be here mostly every two weeks while he was at Fort Hood. He and his brother were stationed at the same place.

While he was gone I mostly did nothing, just sat around and looked at soap operas. Sometimes, chopping cotton. Me and my sister-in-law would take turns babysitting the kids alternating days going to the field.

My first child, James, was born in June 1974. I was living with his mama. My time caring for children before this was no more than taking care of my nieces, my oldest sister's girls and the sister next to me, her girls. With James it wasn't like playing with dolls, I know that. It was exciting, never a dull moment, at nighttime they would be crying but I got over it, it wasn't a problem. I have four children now, two daughters and two sons.

With my first child, my mother-in-law wouldn't let me sleep with him, he slept with her until he was three months old. She told me I didn't know nothing about sleeping with no baby, I'd be done mashed him. I told her, "Mama I ain't gonna mash him." But no, he slept with her three months. Then he started sleeping with me. She'd come in and check to see that he was all right.

James is in Texas now; he was staying in Little Rock. When he graduated from high school in 1992, he left and took up electronics technology at the Vo-Tech school in Little Rock. He's an electrician, stayed in Little Rock a couple years and moved to Texas last year, he, his girlfriend and little girl. He called me last night to tell me they were having a small wedding on Saturday, nothing big.

My second child was born in August of 1976, a girl named Caprina. Oh, I was a pro then, she weighed eight pounds and ten ounces. She was the biggest one. My first two was born at the University Hospital in Little Rock. My third one was born at home with a mid-wife attending and my fourth was born at Jefferson Memorial hospital in Dumas.

With my third in 1978 with the mid-wife it was at my mother's house out in the country. That was something I wanted to experience for myself. I had heard other ladies talking about they had so many kids at home until I decided that I was gonna have mine at home. I don't think I wanna go through that no more though.

I thought the baby would never get here. It had come a snow storm in Gould a week or two before and I just knew that she was gonna come with all that ice on the ground, wires and trees covered with ice. But when she was born all of that had melted away.

I got up that Friday morning, I didn't eat breakfast, I wasn't hurting, I just didn't feel right. Around about 10:00 a.m I started hurting. My daddy was getting ready to go get the mid-wife then my husband pulled up from work in the car and he went and got the mid-wife. She was born about 3:15 p.m. I had more pain than before. She was eight pounds and three ounces. I sure was glad when that was over with and I said, "I'll never do this no more."

I have three grandbabies, one six, one eight in August, and one turned nine in April. My second daughter is about to have a baby and she's drawing a Social Security disability check. My other daughter is about to have a baby too. She works at Tyson's. My youngest son who just graduated from Dumas High School is in the Navy and in Atlanta, Georgia at Morehouse College.

I wanted to become a beautician, I wanted to do hair. But after I finished school, I decided to get married, stay at home and have babies. I didn't think

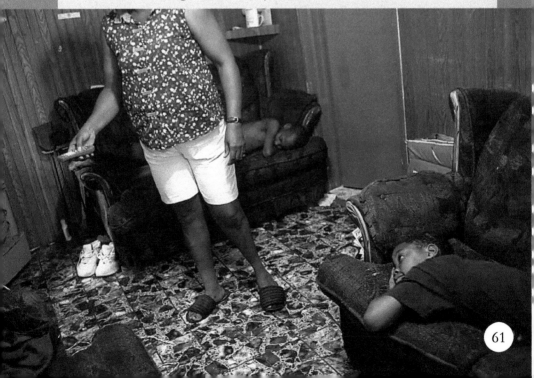

of no beautician classes or nothing. I just stayed at home and had babies. Then I decided, since my husband didn't want to work too often, I had to go get a job and support the family. He didn't want me to work but I went on anyway, somebody had to support the family. I was twenty-three years old and had three young children.

I went to the unemployment office and I filled out an application. Dantan sewing factory called me for an interview at the job and they hired me that day. I started working at the sewing factory in November of 1979. I went to my machine, I was sorta nervous 'cause I'd never been in a factory before. They gave me a little scrap piece to sew on to get use to the machine, the speed and all that stuff. I sewed all day and next day and I started setting sleeves. We sewed on blouses, pants and dresses and some days we hemmed shorts. I went to work at 7 a.m. and worked until 3:30 p.m. We got off from 11 a.m. to 12 p.m. for lunch. At that time I brought my lunch, later I started eating at Catfish Kitchen or Sonic.

We had chairs in there and we wore an apron over our clothes to keep the thread and stuff off. The little machine thing would slide and bring a box of shirts you set on the floor. There were people in front of me, behind me and on the side. We weren't allowed to talk, but we talked anyway. We had a supervisor and she would come by and speak. If we needed anything we would either stand up or wave our hand, she'd come and see what we want.

In this job I had no health insurance, no sick days, and no retirement. If I'd catch a cold or something like that, I'd take two Tylenol and go on to work. I ain't never been seriously sick. We got paid vacation, a week for Fourth of July, Christmas and off on Memorial and Labor Days. I got paid every week.

You couldn't say the word union at this factory. Now what thing the union is, I don't really know. Some folks came by there one year, union folks, but they wouldn't allow us to talk to them. We wanted a union but if we'd talk to them folks, we'd probably get fired so nobody talked to them or signed the petition to have a union. The people at the factory didn't want it, didn't approve of it. The owners of the factory run them folks away.

I worked almost fourteen years setting sleeves and side seams. I worked on until the plant went out of business in 1993.

Next, I drawed unemployment for one month. Through the unemployment office in Dumas I called and went down for an interview and then I went to work August 30, 1993, with Bassett furniture upholstery factory. We started off sewing like at the other factory, sewing a little scrap piece. You'd get use to the speed of the machine and we started sewing on pillows to go on the couch.

At Bassett I did upholstery, sewing on living room furniture. We did couches, loveseats, reclining chairs, regular chairs and footstools. I got paid every week. I worked in the sewing department from 1993 to February 2000 and it went out of business. I did get severance pay here.

I drawed unemployment from March on 'til September 2002. I drawed all my money and I sit around the house and do nothing but babysit. Some workers at Gould's high school retired so I put in an application there and I was hired. I stayed there until the school went out of business and then I went to Reed Elementary School in Dumas.

I work as custodian at the school from 3 p.m. to 11 p.m. Monday through Friday. I clean the bathroom and mop it. I make sure they have enough tissue, paper towels and soap, get the marks off the wall if any up there, sweep the classrooms, empty waste baskets, change plastic bags in the waste baskets and mop floors.

We get retirement and vacation time and sick leave. I have life insurance, no health insurance. If I go to the doctor I have to pay cash right then and there, no health card. I get paid once a month. I get paid more money now and I got more bills. But so far I ain't had anything cut off. Some of my bills are due on the first of the month, some on the tenth and some on the twenty-third. I usually budget paying my bills.

I trust in God. I trust that He gives me the knowledge and ability to understand. Things happen in life that you can't explain and you look to Him for guidance and strength and wisdom. It's a lot of things that you don't understand and it might not be for me to understand but He is good to me.

I call on God to help me. Sometimes when I get a shut-off notice for the lights or water and instead of me paying the bill off, I go and buy something else, I say, "Oh Lord, this man goin' to turn my lights off, what am I going to do?" I would call and he'd give me a few more days to pay my bill and I'd say, "Thank God." I never lost faith, I always believe He'll never fail me, never let me down.

I may have let myself down but He ain't never let me down.

If I was talking to young women, I would tell them to put God first. If you put Him first everything else will fall in line. Understand, keep your head up, don't let nothing stress you out, frustrate you, make you feel sad, be happy, put your hand in God's hand and everything will be all right.

Jericho on Highway 114 is my home church, my father and mother belonged there too. It's the tradition church for my family. As a child, Sunday School started at 9:30 a.m. and we would always be on time regardless of the weather, whether or not we had money to put in, mother would still get us up to go. I enjoyed Sunday School, I go now, I went last Sunday.

In Sunday School we learn about the Bible, Jesus Christ, God, the way you live, the way not to live, things about life that will make you strong when you get weak, encourage you, keep your head up, make you feel like if something bad happen to you it won't last always, good things are coming to those who wait for it. You must be patient, it takes time and everything will be all right.

Sometimes you have some things in life you go through, you say, "well Lord, you said it'll be over after awhile and in a few days it'll be over with" and you go on and forget it. I don't let things bother me too much if I can avoid it. If I have to go through it, I just have to go through it and with the Lord's help He'll bring me out. I know that Jesus will fix it. It might not be when I get ready but He'll be there on time, all I have to do is wait.

We don't have but few adults that go to our church now. Most of them have died. The oldest member of our church is my uncle and he's ninety-four. There's about fifteen of us. Rev. Harris is our pastor, he's full time. He encourages us to keep the faith and especially to love one another and just be friendly, trust in the Lord. He tells us that every Sunday. Be of good courage and everything'll be all right.

My mother had influence on me. She died in 1993. She was a good person, I miss her and she always told us, "Do good in school, try to do the best you can; keep on living and keep on keeping on." She'd talk to me about getting rest because I was always up doing something or doing something for somebody.

She was like that. If somebody was to call her and wanted her to do something, she would go. If she had aches and pains, she never complained about nothing. We never did know it unless she stood up and said, "Oh my hip's hurting" or side or something like that. She would think that we didn't know it but if they wanted to borrow some money, she would give it to them. While we were looking she'd try to ease it to them like we didn't know. We never said anything but we would know it. If they paid or not paid it back, it was all right, she didn't worry about anything like that.

She always told us, "Always help somebody no matter what color because one day you might need help from somebody, help don't come in no color when you need help, you just need it."

I'm like her in some ways. She was a little taller and brighter than I am. She had brown eyes, gold teeth and wore glasses. She wore her hair combed back and an apron everyday. I think our personalities and attitudes toward people are just alike. She got along with everybody, male, female, black or white, she was a friendly lady. I think I'm like that. A smile never hurt no one, to me.

She was a religious woman, she got us ready to go to Sunday School every Sunday and to church. She would get us ready for school daily, cook our breakfast, we'd eat if we wanted to and she'd have supper ready for us in the evenings. She told us to learn all we can and learn to like everybody, and don't be picky about helping folks, just love everybody.

It's quiet and peaceful here, not too much trouble occur here.

You might have a few break-ins sometimes, other than that it's quiet and peaceful. Nobody bothers nobody, everybody knows everybody, everybody's neighbors.

Clora T. Green

My grandson stays with me. He turned twelve years old this month, last Wednesday, he's in the fifth grade. He goes to school at the school where I work. He's been there a year, almost two years. We live in a house behind the apartments. We were staying in a trailer. My sister-in-law had a house, I asked her where she got it from, she told me about this company in Pine Bluff called "Happy Home." I got in touch with them to see what I could do to get me a house like the one she had. They told me I needed a $200 deposit. I made the deposit and they brought the house and set it on my lot – two bedrooms, kitchen, bathroom, living room. The bathroom already had the tub, stool, sink and the kitchen had the cabinets, I sure was glad. We got the house in 1981 with a house note and moved in.

It's a big responsibility. I have to budget my money. It's hard when I get paid and my bills are more than my money is. Then I have to pay half on this one and half on that one and pay one in full, but things always work out smoothly. I've never had any cut-offs. You have to keep the bills paid, keep the house up, and make sure no one throws rocks and break windows, leave the water running in the winter time so your pipes don't burst. It needs a paint job now, other than that, it's alright.

I feel secure because it's mine, something I own myself. Renting is renting forever but paying for it, it's your own property. I've paid it off. I've bought it; it's my little shack.

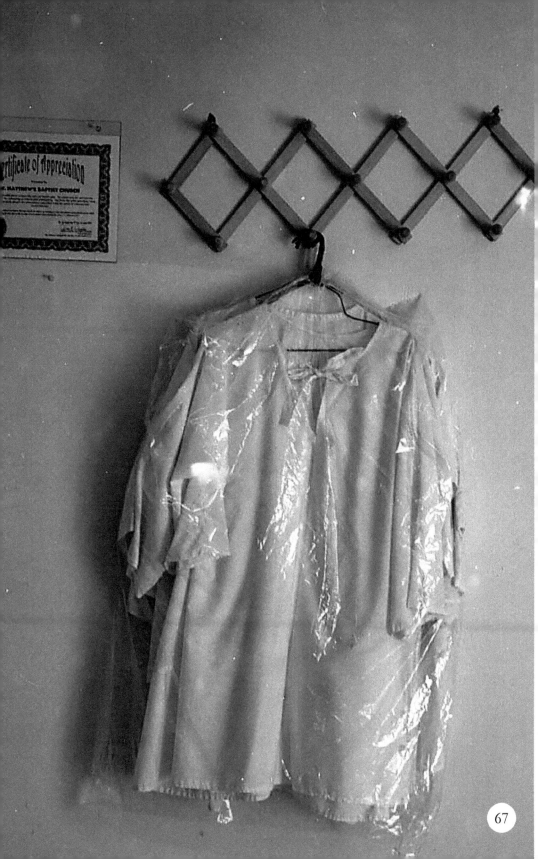

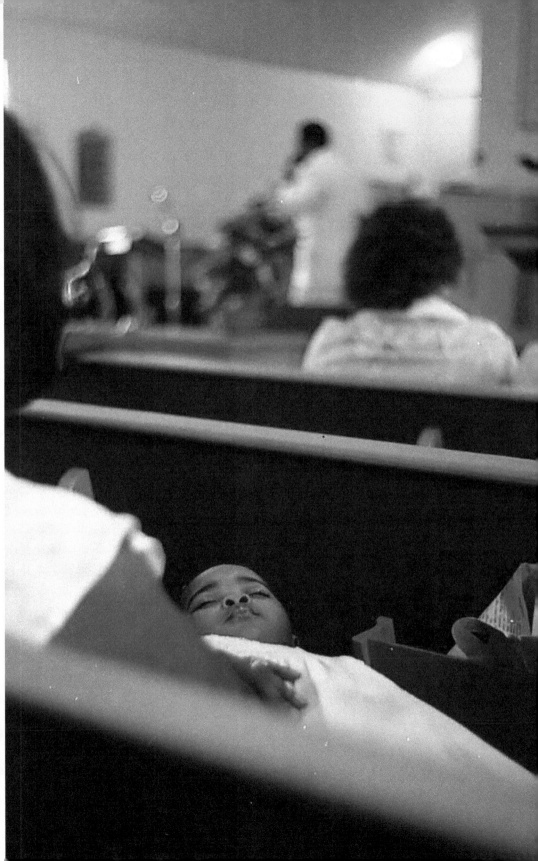

Beatrice Clark Shelby

I lived in Trenton, Arkansas, a small community and it's about two hundred people. It's eight miles from Marvell. I was living with my mother, a brother and a sister on a place called the Castle farm. We lived in a very large house. There was a peach orchard out there, we had gardens and we had barns. Peaches, apricots, peppers, grapes, all kinds of fruits. We rented the house and the land from the Castle family that owned the farm.

We spent our time chopping and picking cotton, slopping the hogs, feeding the chickens, and I always found time to read, I loved to read. We canned and pieced quilts. I used to make my clothes. To preserve meat, we used to put salt on it. My mother always canned beef. She would put it in a sack, take a lot of meat, grind it up, put it in a jar and hang it up. I am not a person that likes meat now. I like vegetables and fruits.

The only really major struggle that I can remember in my life was between the time I graduated from high school in May 1966, until I entered into business school, the same year.

Well, my momma always wanted her children to have an education. She just felt that the next generation should always do better. When my mama came along, if you got an eighth grade education you could probably teach. She did not get to eighth grade I don't think. It was something mama wanted us to have, a school diploma and we worked hard to make sure we got it. When I was growing up parents actually concentrated more on education that they do these days. A black family, in particular, would always talk about the way out of poverty for the children was education.

I rode the school bus from Trenton to Marvell to M.M. Tate High School. It was not integrated. High school was not a real good experience for me. I've always been a good reader. Most of the time, I think that was my problem, I would sit back and just read. I did not interact and do all that playing with folks. I didn't run all over the school and go to dances and stuff like that, was not in the band, or none of the extracurricular activities at school. When I hear people talk about high school, it was "get through it." I graduated from Marvell High School in May 1966. We had graduation ceremonies, commencement exercises, all of those things. Probably about forty students graduated.

One thing that I always thought about during my junior and senior year was that I wanted to go to Arkansas Baptist College because I'd heard people talk about it. Arkansas Baptist College, Philander Smith and Shorter College were all African American schools in Little Rock. Those were the colleges you knew about because you went to church. That was during the Civil Rights Movement, a lot of things were going on relating to that. People encouraged you to go to college.

My mom wanted her children to go to college. The very next year, my sister went to Mary Holmes College in Mississippi and my oldest brother went there also. My auntie lived in Mississippi and most of her children went on to college so that was something I wanted to do.

The struggle in my life was that I wanted to go to Arkansas Baptist College and I could not figure out how to get into college. I don't think that my grades were bad or anything. I just did not know how to work the process or surround myself with the people that could have helped me to get in. I talked to my mama about this and she did not know how to work the process either.

Well most of the time, you have to be accepted, whatever the requirements were I did not do it, so I knew I wasn't going. The bottom line is if you don't know how to work the system, you just don't work it. You feel very frustrated when you can't get to point B from point A but I wasn't angry about it or with someone else. I felt like if I really wanted to do it I should have started early and it was something I should have been able to do.

A lot of children in my class during that time period went on to college. My self-confidence at that time was pretty good. Basically I don't let things really worry me, either I can do 'em or not do 'em and move on to something else. But really at that point I really wanted to do that and I couldn't figure out how to do it. That was probably the only time and the first time in my life I felt powerless.

I guess my empowered moments of building me as a human being probably came between 1968 and 1972. From when I was eighteen to twenty-five years old, Fannie Mae Turner, youth advisor at Pleasant Grove Church, my church, Margaret Staub of Mid Delta Community Services, and John Hamilton, active in NAACP, became my role models.

In Helena some guy that worked for a furniture company had gotten killed, in some relation to the police, I don't know how but the guy ended up dead. John Hamilton decided that he was going to march. Mr. Hamilton was a carpenter in the Marvell area at one time and I understand that he did something displeasing to the white community and therefore they no longer would let him work on their houses. Margaret Staub or Jim Murphy who was director of the Office of Economic Opportunity hired him and Fannie Turner.

I noticed that people did not always tell the truth on Mr. Hamilton. They would just outright tell lies about what he was doing. He used to say, "I can't hear what you're saying for looking at what you're doing." He really showed me how people could see you one way and you were another way. We really had to try to do what is right. If they said something about us, we tried to make sure it wasn't a lie. Those were things that I learned from John Hamilton.

Mrs. Fannie Mae Turner, youth advisor at my church, had called us. She said we all needed to go march in protest with Mr. Hamilton because the people wouldn't fire all of us from our jobs. This has always stayed with me. Fannie Mae Turner was very courageous. She would do things that other folks would be afraid to do. She would take chances. She was very protective and cared about Mr. Hamilton's job.

Now the reason John Hamilton became a role model for me during that time period is because he would always do things and try to fight for the people's civil rights, was real active in the NAACP.

I found out about this group [NAACP] through Fannie. She was going to a meeting one night and asked me to come go with her and that's just how I got started. Then I had this one gentleman, whose name was Ellis McKissic. He was an older deacon at my church. He loved to go to the meetings but had gotten so he could not drive that well. So if he wanted to go to Marianna or wherever to NAACP meetings, I would take him and I enjoyed and learned so much from him.

They just met around the table and talked about things they wanted to do. We probably met at a church. That was my first experience in organizing and thinking about what tomorrow's gonna bring. Those people organized. They talked about what they wanted to do to help people. They were truly NAACP members. You got a chance to go to regional, state and national conventions. I was in my early twenties and was living in Trenton with my mom.

At that time NAACP members were doing some training. I became a part of that group and started traveling with Mrs. Fannie. I felt like I was really making progress. They were training me to have some life coping skills and that you could make a difference. I think that's the one time in my life, working with them and watching them do things, I felt we really could make a difference. They had this group called Phillips County Community Action Club.

When I think about that march, we were out there marching down the street, they could have killed us. During that march, Fannie really thought about John Hamilton, so it stayed with me that she cared about his job, not about her job. It didn't make him any difference, he was gonna march whatever, but she wanted to try to protect his job by putting enough of us out there that the person wouldn't fire all of us. I don't happen to believe that she would have fired anybody but that was Mrs. Turner.

I remember we were marching. As I look back, people could have gotten shot. I didn't think about it when I was marching because we were out there and doing what we thought was right but it was dangerous. I guess I did stuff because I felt that it needed to be done. I marched because I felt that we needed to march.

The NAACP really made me feel that I was part of a group that wanted to make some positive changes. These folks were for real, not for show. Mrs. Fannie always took the children on trips. The thing that stood out was how she had the youth involved. When my daughter was like nine or ten years old she did a speech. I can see the children doing some speeches and things now, they actually was prepared.

Margaret Staub, another mentor, was and is today, the Executive Director at Mid-Delta Community Services, a community action agency. She came from Scotland. She was real young at that time so she would always talk about how you would do things right. I liked to be around her 'cause if you did something that was not correct, she would take the pen and red marker and make corrections. That was how Margaret mentored me because if something was wrong we needed to straighten it out before it went any further.

In November of 1967 Mid Delta Community Services hired me. They had the Head Start program, a good program that teaches small children with a parenting component that helps. It also has the emergency food and medical program, weatherization, transportation programs. So it helps the people in the community to meet their needs.

The next experience I had that made me think we could really make a difference, we met to try to build a housing complex in Poplar Grove. We were a group of people called Poplar Grove Rural Development Housing project and I was on that board. People were saying that we would never build a housing complex, however Farmer's Home, U.S. Department of Agriculture did build a housing complex. The housing project is still there, built in 1969.

I moved into the project the first year. I lived in house number fifteen, the second brick house from the end, with my mother, oldest brother, and Draco, my oldest nephew. It was a seventeen-house project.

When I was growing up, we did not have brick houses. You just had houses that had tin on it. We always did wall paper every year. We put down linoleum just about every year. We washed clothes by hand until probably in the early sixties. We made soap. To make soap they took out the tallow or fat from the beef and put lye in it and put it in a pot and boiled it so it could make soap.

FOR IMMEDIATE RELEASE
September 3, 2020
Becky Williams
PO Box 250804
Little Rock, AR 72225
Rcwilliams715@yahoo.com

SOWING SEEDS OF JUSTICE

Courage, Persistence and Faith of African American Women in the Delta

This book of interviews and photographs features ten African American women of stature and grace from east Arkansas, selected and documented through a community oral history project. Author and editor Becky Williams asked each woman to describe a life experience or crisis where she felt distressed, oppressed, hopeless or helpless; a second experience where she felt the competency and power to make decisions in her life and create more equity in her community; and what happened during her life that helped her change. Each woman chose the experiences she wanted

SOWING SEEDS
OF JUSTICE

Courage, Persistence and Faith
of African American Women of the Delta

Becky Williams, Editor
Laurent Guerin, Photographer

This book gives voice to black women activists in the Arkansas Delta whose stories have remained largely unheard and marginalized. Jean Davis, a factory worker, union leader and former sharecropper in 1960's east Arkansas travels to the 1981 Labor Day rally in Washington DC. Gertrude Jackson tells about standing in hallways flowing with sewage in Marvell's new "separate but equal" school for blacks in 1960's. She tells of the battle she and her husband waged through the courts for integrated education in the Marvell School District.

Others can now use the example of these women's lives as tools for change in organizing and moving people to action. The women made choices in their lives and lived with the consequences. They used their values of love and compassion to direct them – they chose to make their lives better and to help those around them.

To support independent local book stores, books may be purchased at Wordsworth Bookstore, 5920 R Street, Little Rock, AR, 501-663-9198, and through their website wordsworthbookstore.com from where they may be shipped nationwide. Books may also be ordered through national outlets.

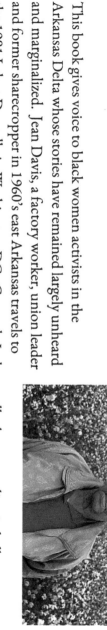

We had outdoor toilets and baths and we pumped water until 1969 when we moved into Poplar Grove houses.

We had been there probably a year in these newly built houses when the sewer started messing up. We had raw sewage coming up on the ground outside the houses. It had a real bad odor.

I held an office in the Poplar Grove Housing Complex at the time the sewer messed up. Everybody that lived in the project elected your president, secretary and treasurer. I moved from the secretary position to the president. I was twenty-one and was working at my first job in the office as a secretary for Mid-Delta Community Services.

Alma Norton was the lady that I went up town to talk to about the sewage system messing up. She worked for Van Meter Lumber Company. I walked into the building and I was explaining to her that the septic tank and sewage system down there was messing up. She proceeded to explain to me that we had torn up the housing project. We, the people who lived in there. Alma Norton was a very nice person. So I was standing there looking at her. My mother just loved this project so that really upset me, to say that my mother and all these people that loved those houses so, had torn them up because they were in perfect condition at that time. It was just the sewer system.

And I think I found my voice then.

I went to talk to John Hamilton, my mentor in the NAACP. We talked and he said, "If you really want to do something about it, get a petition and send it to…" I don't know if it was Senator Bumpers or Governor Bumpers at that time.

That's what we decided after talking to John Hamilton. He told me the one thing that was gonna be real hard was to get the people in the project to sign the petition. It wasn't difficult at all because I really worked hard to get everyone to sign the petition. It wasn't the idea that I was doing so much. Once we got people to sign up, they actually continued their support. I've heard people say that people will put you out on a limb by yourself, but in this instance, they did not put me out there by myself, they really supported. So they sent Ollie Neal, who is Judge Ollie Neal now, down to help us with the Poplar Grove housing project. He worked for the Lee County Cooperative Clinic. It was Ollie Neal and two or three more people that came down to Poplar Grove and worked with us and we managed to get the project's system put in place.

My thing about finding voices is the same thing with leadership. During that time period from 1968 to probably 1972, I had all these people, that when I sent to them they were always willing to help. But I knew at that time that I had to put forth a lot of effort. I think I went back to school in 1970 at the college.

So this was my first taste of really being in power, that if you worked hard at something you can get it done.

Now, my first thing is to read the Bible. I have two sisters that I study the Bible with. My oldest sister who lives in Nashville, Tennessee, we get on the phone and study the Bible together and my sister in Helena, Arkansas we read the Bible together. My favorite scripture by far is the sixth chapter of Matthew and the thirty-third verse, "Seek ye first the kingdom of God and his righteousness and all other things will be added unto you."

When I came to BGACDC in 1982, I remember having that little card that someone sent to me. I remember sticking it up in the door; it was on a little brown card. I still have that sign in my office.

I go to a Baptist church so our children went to Sunday school and church. We have the same pastor we've had for about thirty-eight years and about fifty people attend service. When you reached twelve years old, we made sure that you got on the mourner's bench so that you would become a child of God. You would sit on that bench and people pray for you and you get off the mourners' bench when you believe that Jesus Christ died on the cross and rose from the dead on the third day.

I feel most empowered when I think about my mother and the things that she taught me. One thing that was hung in our house all the time was the Ten Commandments on a blue card sprinkled with glitter. In some ways I'm very different from my mother because I'm a little more out spoken about things, I will mingle and I'm more out-going than her. I'm not as smart academically as my mother was even though she did not complete high school.

However, both of us have that thirst for knowledge. Both my mother and I wanted to pass information and traditions down to our children. My mother always prayed over her children and I pray a lot for my children. We're very protective of our children and want the best for them. Another thing, my mother always tried to help in the community – I think I try to help in the community.

I had all these mentors, John Hamilton, Margaret Staub and Fannie Turner, and they led by example. I tried to associate myself with people that I saw doing stuff that I felt was going to impact the community. They were a different breed of people than most. They knew what they wanted to do, they wanted to make a positive change and they did not sit back and wait for someone else to do it. What came out of their mouths was what they did. They took action to try to make things different. They would go and get people, take them to the food stamp office and help them to fill out papers.

This was one of the reasons I got my notary license years ago because a lot of folks needed notarization and people would charge them. So you go get your license and charge the minimum fee according to the law, therefore, you would help folks. As I got older and learned how, when people needed papers filled out to go to the food stamp or Social Security offices, I would do those things because it was leading by example.

After working at Mid Delta, I had the opportunity to come to Boys, Girls, Adults Community Development Center (BGACDC), the parent organization of Delta Women Achieving Goals and Delta Youth Achieving Goals. It is a grassroots organization located in eastern Arkansas. Over twenty-five years ago committed parents living in the town of Marvell came together to save their children and created BGACDC. Because of my role models and the teamwork that I learned from Mid Delta and NAACP, when I came to BGACDC I felt confident that if we worked together we could make a difference and we did.

The reason I have changed is because when you do something and you do not get the results that you expect then you have to change, you're not going to continue to do the same things over and over again. A book that greatly influenced my life is *Who Moved My Cheese*. You don't just sit there and wait, you deal with change. You had two little people and two little mice, they all had cheese. When they ran out of cheese, the two people waited around and the mice went out and looked for more.

So it says you deal with change, you don't just wait around.

My younger son called the other night, and it was so strange. He's just twenty-four. He said that the more he sees people, he really feels like we did a good job raising him. And I told him I got a few more years, so I will agree at this point.

To know me, you would know a servant. That's how I see myself, as someone to serve someone else. I hope that when I'm gone that the people that actually knew me can truly say that Beatrice Shelby strove to make a positive difference in the Delta. I hope that I have lived such a life, that I am a good neighbor, that I served my neighbors, and that I help people when I can.

Chesa Owens

Chesa Owens

There was a time in my life when I experienced a very hard, oppressed time. Most everybody including black and white were without money, it was hard. When you had a neighbor, then if you got low in food or had some kind of medical problem, they helped. Most time the churches in the neighborhood would pitch in, give dollars, fifty cents and make up enough money to pay for medicine or get you to a doctor.

I can remember one time in my life when we was really, really down. I was somewhere along about twelve or fourteen years old in the early 1960's. I hadn't graduated yet. Those were very depressing times. We were living out in the country. The white farmer owned the land. Sharecropping means you gave him…it's a fifty/fifty thing. You raised the farm and he got half of whatever you made. We raised, weeded, and chopped cotton and soybeans. If you didn't make enough for that half of what he was supposed to get, then he took it all. So sharecropping was a bad deal. It was a bad thing for the poor, most times they would fix it so that you wouldn't clear. You were never gonna clear as long as you're sharecropping.

You'd always be in debt to that man that gave you the loan to farm with. We had a house but he owned the land. He may have rented from someone else but it was under his jurisdiction. You can say he owned it because it wasn't ours.

Our house had two front doors and two back doors. We had all wood floors, no rugs. I remember my dad purchasing all wood floors that had to be put together. We had to fix the house when we moved in. We did the wallpaper, the wallpaper was not like it is today, you used tacks, the wide head shiny tacks. You'd cut the paper out in little squares and stick the tack through it to make it. Back in those times we had to do that and put something on because there was one wall in the house, an outside wall and the other wall, no insulation, nothing like that. There was no television in our house, my dad didn't want a television and we had no electricity.

Then we had our personal gardens, like we raised produce for the farmer's market. We had one horse and one mule. Our garden would go out in February. Dad would get the Irish potatoes and red potatoes out. We had like a half-acre of sweet peas, they would come off early. We raised our own sugar cane, had our own eggs. We started canning as soon as the stuff was ready. Canning would probably start somewhere long about March. You had to get the jars ready so when the stuff would come off, the jars would be ready. If we'd do the sweet peas on Thursday, we'd do the canning on Friday. It didn't take sweet peas long to cook, we canned dozens and dozens of jars of sweet peas.

We took the sorghum to Mr. Ivory Tillman's sorghum grinder and he took them off and made syrup, and we also had sorghum to sell. They made this syrup and we sold some of that – molasses. My dad sold that to help us eat during those months of non-farm time. We raised stuff to put in jars. My mom would always do seventy or eighty quarts of vegetables and things from our garden, all that we didn't sell. We had to save some of it for cash money. There was squash, green beans, okra, cantaloupe preserves, watermelon preserves, purple hull peas, jelly made from purple hull peas, peaches of which we made jelly from the hull. We didn't throw away anything.

The women didn't go to the farmer's market. The boys and my daddy went. Me, my sisters, and mom was at home. At home I washed the jars and made sure there was no cracked places, lids and jars clean and stir contents of the iron pot. We always had a couple of pots and you made your fire outside to keep from heating the house up. We had no electricity. We had to put up so many green beans, speckled butter beans, corn so while we were shelling the peas and beans, my mom would be cutting the corn off the cob. There was a lot of things going on at one time and everyone had something to do. And there was no pleasure, no fun. We worked because you had to have your food ready for the winter. This food was canned for the winter months when stuff was all gone in the garden.

During the winter we lost a lot of the jars 'cause some of the jars burst, we couldn't keep them warm enough. In our house, we had four beds. Every bed would be packed with jars underneath. We had to put 'em somewhere in the house where they could stay warm but we lost a lot of stuff. It was so cold they froze. The houses were not like these today.

There were seven of us, my mom, dad, four brothers and sisters. We was working, call it sharecropping or renting land and getting our loan money from Mr. H. During that year, we worked in our fields and soybeans and cotton didn't make enough to pay off our loan bill at the end of the year. This was a bad year for farming. The boll weevils ate up the crops. So there was not enough money to pay the people to spray with airplanes. We got it sprayed but not enough. Times were hard.

My mom and dad was sitting around the eating table talking about it. So I told, see I was the second oldest in my family, so I told my brother which is David,

"You know what, we gonna starve to death."

He said, "Naw, you know daddy, he always find a way, mama, they not gonna let us starve."

This was the end of harvesting time, September, October, November, December, before Christmas holidays. You got your crops out of the field, you done sold and you see that you not gonna clear so they sat around talking about it. All your resources and you don't have any more to give. You don't have money, you can't clear your bills that you borrowed the money for. See you borrowed the money to farm on. You can't clear your bills to pay for your seeds you put in the ground. You can't pay for the half of the crop you raised, you don't have enough money to pay, there's no way out.

I thought we was gonna starve. A lot of people they was talking about had starved to death.

I can remember daddy saying, "I don't know what we're gonna eat and how we're gonna eat, they're foreclosing on us." They was taking what we had earned to pay off the bill, and still it wasn't enough. But daddy gave it to them without having anything, not a penny left. We gave that to 'em.

I remember my mom saying her prayers, "Lord, I don't know how I'm gonna feed my kids. I got five children and a husband and this man is taking our chickens, hogs, everything." That meant that we weren't gonna have food, shelter, nowhere to go. This man, Mr. H., never came once to say, "I'm sorry you got children, I don't want those children to starve." He didn't say anything, you either pay or get out.

Some people came over and talked to my dad and said, "Well why don't you go talk to Mr. Trotter? He's helped quite a few black farmers." My dad said,

"Aw, ain't no need." Mama said, "Go! Just go!" So I remember my dad telling my mom, "Get in this old truck, c'mon let's go to Monticello. I know a man who used to help people." It was this white gentleman whose name is Mr. Trotter. He helped a lot of people, you know over in Monticello, Arkansas. So my mom and dad left us all at home.

They went on out there, came back, momma jumped out the truck, she said, "Oh thank you Lord! Halleluiah! Thank you Lord!" We started jumping too 'cause from all the action, there must have been something that went on good in Monticello.

So we got money, he gave my daddy over thousands and thousands of dollars to pay off that loan, to Mr. H. off so we could have money to purchase food and clothing and do whatever including gas because we had a 1940 Model T. I remember my daddy going to purchase a lot of food and clothing, coal for the heater, we had a coal burning heater.

When Mr. Trotter gave my dad the money, we got the cows back. See when he gave him the loan, we repurchased those animals back because when Mr. H. took them from us, he said he took them to sell. He actually didn't sell them, so Mr. Trotter went and got 'em back from him for us. The Trotters helped Daddy do a lot of things once he got out of bondage of Mr. H.

Let me tell you about my daddy trying to make me go to college. He went down to Merchants and Farmers bank and borrowed eight thousand dollars to make me go to University of Arkansas Pine Bluff. I did not wanna go, that's why I signed up to go to the U.S. Marines because I didn't wanna go to college. I told my dad, "I'm not a college person." I barely got out of high school. I was slow. He said, "You can go, they got tutors." I said, "I'm not going to college, you just take that eight thousand dollars back down there and give it to them."

My dad and I sat down and talked about it, he said, "Okay then, you don't wanna go to college, do whatever you wanna do. Be a decent person, work. Be a decent person, not a drunk, run around all night out all times of the night 'cause in this house when 12:00 a.m. comes that door gonna be locked. You can be twenty-one if you're still here, you can't come in after 12:00 a.m. You can be twenty-five, if you're still here, you cannot come in here after twelve, in my house." I'm glad my dad did that for me.

My dad said, "There's a factory job out there and they do hire people when you graduate from high school." I told him I was scared to go out there 'cause I'd never been to a factory, never gone to town a lot of times, my dad always did the shopping, mom and dad. He said, "Just go out there, you'll see, just put an application in." So I went, signed up for the civil service exam. My daddy took me and I didn't pass that.

He said, "There's things for young black people to do, do it." He took me

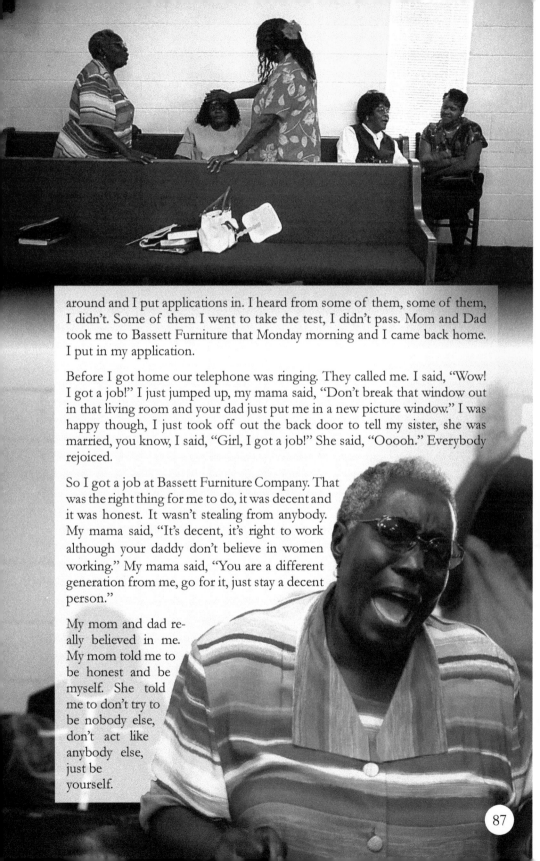

around and I put applications in. I heard from some of them, some of them, I didn't. Some of them I went to take the test, I didn't pass. Mom and Dad took me to Bassett Furniture that Monday morning and I came back home. I put in my application.

Before I got home our telephone was ringing. They called me. I said, "Wow! I got a job!" I just jumped up, my mama said, "Don't break that window out in that living room and your dad just put me in a new picture window." I was happy though, I just took off out the back door to tell my sister, she was married, you know, I said, "Girl, I got a job!" She said, "Ooooh." Everybody rejoiced.

So I got a job at Bassett Furniture Company. That was the right thing for me to do, it was decent and it was honest. It wasn't stealing from anybody. My mama said, "It's decent, it's right to work although your daddy don't believe in women working." My mama said, "You are a different generation from me, go for it, just stay a decent person."

My mom and dad really believed in me. My mom told me to be honest and be myself. She told me to don't try to be nobody else, don't act like anybody else, just be yourself.

She instilled the word of the Lord in us, we was churchgoing folks, we had to go. Even when my mom and dad didn't go, they would always send me. She told me, "Just because you're black don't mean you're nobody. You are somebody, so act like somebody. Don't act like you see some people act. There's such things as people drinking, you don't need to do that."

So I didn't have a drink till I was about twenty years old. My mama told me you can be somebody. My daddy called me "black gal." He said, "Black gal, you can do whatever you wanna do. Just don't get no babies. Nobody's having babies in this house but me and your mama and we're not having any more."

Now I would tell young people who said, "I'm really struggling in my life," I would tell them to take a period, a moment to sit down and think about it. Think about what it is you want to do. Go and talk to somebody who has already walked in those shoes that you're about to embark upon. Let them know what it is you want to do.

Talk to someone you believe in that you can do anything you wanna do. Someone told me some years later, you don't have to be a genius, you don't have to have a master's degree or be a college graduate student to do whatever you need to do to make life better and those people that surround you. I would tell them to keep their goal in mind. Somewhere along in life, you will accomplish it. Technology has advanced so if you keep studying, keep looking at that thing you wanna do, you can do it. Don't give up.

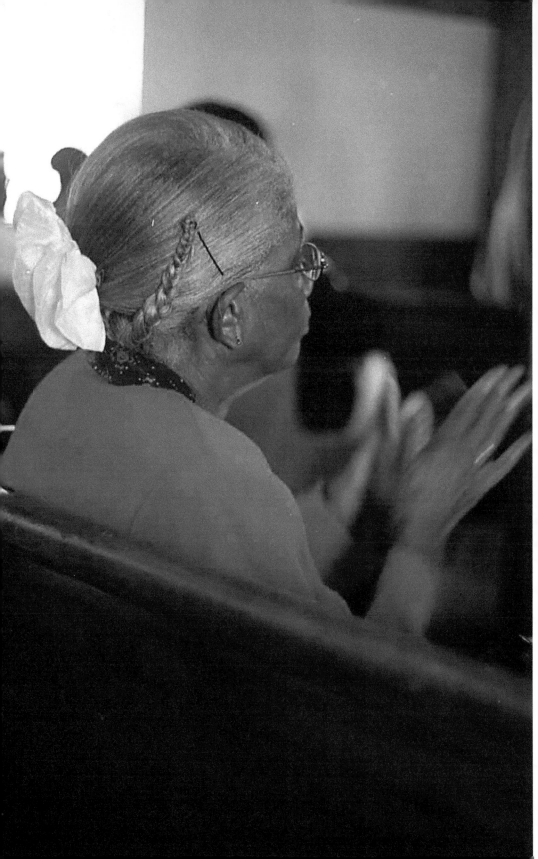

Cora Nash

I think the thing that depressed me most in my life was the death of my third child. I was twenty-seven years old. You know you want all of your children but the pregnancy came at a time that I really needed something to hope for.

My family has always been my passion. They're my life, that's what I lived for and that's what I live for now. I have in the past, gotten up in the morning thinking, "What would make my family happy?" I cleaned my house to make my husband proud. I did the meal when we were at the beginning stage where I took one chicken and made two or three meals out of it. The table had to be set nice and meal look attractive and it had to taste good, made no difference that we were so poor at one stage.

I don't think it's anything wrong with being devoted to your family but some-times I think we, out of our devotion, misfocus. Rather than focusing some of my energy on me, I had directed all of my energy towards my husband and my children. I don't regret that at all, it's just that I should have focused on me some too. Then my husband got involved in other things and decided that he wanted to leave and he left with my love and my blessing.

At that period when my baby died, we had separated. When he left, he left not knowing that I was pregnant because I didn't know. I was so irregular with my periods. I would be three and four months before I would realize it and I was not quite three months pregnant when he left. When I did find out, I asked that he not come back because I didn't want that to be the reason, so he didn't come back but we remained friends.

It seems as though during the entire pregnancy I took so good care of myself even more so than ever before, not that the others weren't wanted.

Seems like I just wanted this baby so bad.

After I had him, he was such an odd baby, it was as though he was already mature at birth, and he did things that newborn babies didn't normally do. His name was Kenneth Malachia. Just over night, he took sick, contracted a respiratory virus. He became sick on Sunday evening. Monday morning at the hospital, he was dead. An older friend sat with me until family came, after my baby died.

He was five weeks and two days old when he died.

I think that was the most depressed time in my life because I didn't want to live, even though I had the other children that I loved dearly and I had my husband and family. Some depressions we get over and some we learn to live with. That's one I learned to live with because it's something fairly regularly that will remind me of him.

My husband was home more regularly then making sure that I was okay because he felt that I was his responsibility. I was hoping everything was going to be like it was before and it wasn't so at that time. When the baby died, I was in somewhat of a limbo, I didn't know where I was in the marriage. Most certainly after the baby died I didn't know where I was with life because, like I said, even with the other children, I just wanted to die.

I think I may have felt with my dying I would have been closer to my baby because my arm hurt where I held his head. I would hear him whimpering and crying like he did when he got hungry. I would hold his picture because I took pictures of him soon after he was born and I just wanted to be with him.

He had been deceased about five weeks and my day was spent just sitting and crying. I would get the other two kids dressed and get them to school as soon as I could because I didn't want them to see me crying. As soon as I would drop my son off, I would drop my daughter off around the corner to pre-school. As soon as my son would get out of the car and wave bye, my tears would start and it was an all day thing. I could barely prepare a meal for them. I would cry until it was time to pick them up. Then I would straighten my face up. My son was real attentive of me, still is and he would say, "Momma, what's wrong," and I would say, "I just woke up." He was almost seven when the baby died. He was kind of aware of what was going on.

My friend Barbara getting me out of that house and going to beauty school saved my sanity. One morning I got up, got dressed, and got the kids off to school. I thought I heard the baby crying and went to the crib, which I hadn't been able to take down yet, and I realized he's not here. I grabbed my purse, went out the door and ended up at a person's home. She really wasn't a good friend but an acquaintance, although at that day became one of my greatest friends. We spoke and would see each other occasionally at church, in the grocery store. "How's the children, how you doing, it's good to see you." Usually her comment to me was, "Your hair is so pretty." We probably became friends out of that compliment. Everybody likes it, especially when you're troubled. Everybody likes to be complimented.

I don't think things happen just per chance in life. I think when Kenneth was crying that morning, it was intended for me to hear him. Barbara Lacey was my friend's name. When I went to her shop that morning, it wasn't by chance. I was directed there. I really believe that God directed me there because other people had talked to me and hadn't been able to reach me.

She ran a beauty shop. I always did my own hair. I needed someone to talk to but I couldn't go in and just say I needed someone to talk to so I asked her if she had time to do my hair. In the process of doing my hair, she asked about the baby. She had not heard. I went on to tell her the story and I cried and she cried with me.

Then she said, "You need something to keep you busy and as good as you do your hair and your girl's hair, you need to be out doing something. Why don't you go to beauty school?" Then she gave me the name, address and telephone number of where she had gone. She said, "She'll just let you be yourself, the days you wanna cry, she'll let you cry and the days you wanna work, she'll let you work, and that'll give you something to do."

The day I went to Barbara's shop, I was suppose to go there. It was my day to think about changing my life for the better rather than sitting around thinking, "Poor me, poor me." When you're at that stage, you don't think that other people have gone through this and they survived. First, you're dealing with all of these feelings and then you start wallowing around in them and I was at that stage. She kinda jolted me to get out of it. She has a way of saying things that, even 'til today, make you see and understand.

She told me how sorry she was that the baby had died but I had two other kids to take care of. I need to get up and get out and do something before I lost my mind. And if no more for my kids, then for myself, I needed to straighten up and get myself together. It worked because I had no indication whatsoever that I was interested in doing hair, and it never, never occurred to me to go to beauty school.

Shortly after he died, I started to school. I enrolled and because of that depression, the trade came about. I took very good care of myself and gained a lot of new friends through my clients. I guess that's one good thing that came out of the depression. I didn't intend to follow through with it though.

I had gone to school about four months, and on Thursday, April 12, I decided that I was going to quit. I knew that morning when I went, that would be my last day. I've always given my husband credit to being so in tune with me. He was sensing this too. On that day, April 12, when I returned home, he had the beauty shop foundation poured. I had no idea he was going to, I had no idea that I would own my own shop.

When I got home that day, drove up on the driveway, there's the foundation already poured on the east end of the driveway, hard and ready to walk on because he had done it early that morning. When I saw that I said, "I can't give up if he has that confidence in me." He had written my name and the date in the concrete so I said, "I've got to go on with this."

After that, it was just a straight shot through and that brought me to where I am today. I enjoyed the twelve years that I did it and still do it with my fam-

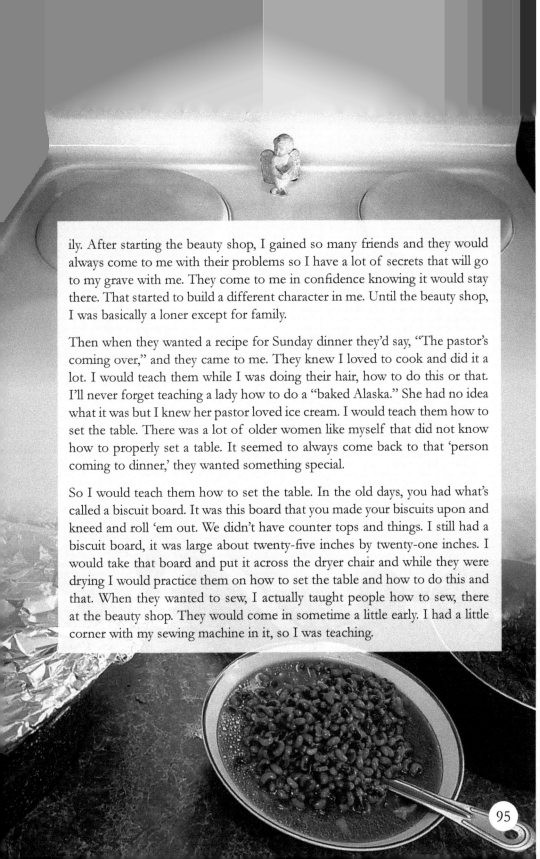

ily. After starting the beauty shop, I gained so many friends and they would always come to me with their problems so I have a lot of secrets that will go to my grave with me. They come to me in confidence knowing it would stay there. That started to build a different character in me. Until the beauty shop, I was basically a loner except for family.

Then when they wanted a recipe for Sunday dinner they'd say, "The pastor's coming over," and they came to me. They knew I loved to cook and did it a lot. I would teach them while I was doing their hair, how to do this or that. I'll never forget teaching a lady how to do a "baked Alaska." She had no idea what it was but I knew her pastor loved ice cream. I would teach them how to set the table. There was a lot of older women like myself that did not know how to properly set a table. It seemed to always come back to that 'person coming to dinner,' they wanted something special.

So I would teach them how to set the table. In the old days, you had what's called a biscuit board. It was this board that you made your biscuits upon and kneed and roll 'em out. We didn't have counter tops and things. I still had a biscuit board, it was large about twenty-five inches by twenty-one inches. I would take that board and put it across the dryer chair and while they were drying I would practice them on how to set the table and how to do this and that. When they wanted to sew, I actually taught people how to sew, there at the beauty shop. They would come in sometime a little early. I had a little corner with my sewing machine in it, so I was teaching.

One day an older friend was making a dress with puffed sleeves, this was back in the seventies, remember now, so puffed sleeves were famous. I was showing her how, she was known to be an expert seamstress but she never could get those sleeves right. That's when it first came into fashion for you to do your basting around the sleeve edge and pull the threads to fit and she had not done this so I was teaching her how to put the puffed sleeves in and she said, "You know, you just teach all the time, you ought to go to school to be a teacher."

As time passed, I kept thinking about it and from January of 1981 to May of 1984, I went to college. After that, teaching built my confidence. Working with the kids that I worked with, you really had to be in control because my six years of teaching was in an all black school in deep south Arkansas. Most of the kids were problems because of one situation or another. Most of them were limited resource kids in every way, resource in finance, knowledge, capability and everything. That was a challenge.

Then I came back home and did not work for a year. I was driving to University of Arkansas in Little Rock three days a week working on my Master's degree when the Cooperative Extension Service called and asked, "Would you like to work for us?" That's what has me here now. Extension has become my job because I work with such a diverse group of people and most of them are limited resource in some way or another. So the teaching position really prepped me for what I'm doing now. The Extension position has become my mission. My mission is my job and my job is my mission.

Working with people and helping people is really what I like to do. It's nice to have a job that you can say, "I get to go to work," rather than, "I have to go or got to go to work." As hectic as it gets, sometimes disgusting, stressful, pressures that you're under meeting deadlines, filling out forms, documenting everything, I still get to go to work because when I can help a person, that's what it's all about.

In my teaching that I do within my job I'm probably a thousand and ten times better off now materialistic than I was coming up. I have so much more.

*I think I buy shoes now because I had to walk to school too many days
two and a half miles to catch the school bus
with cardboard box in the bottom of my shoes for the sole.*

I think I went through that and all the other things that I can show and demonstrate to other people that this is how you can be resourceful, save, supplement, make your home.

My husband and I had a wood floor in our first home. I don't mean hardwood. I'm having hardwood installed now. I thought about it last night, "Why would you want hardwood floors as many wood floors as you've had?" We had a bare wood floor that we painted and then I would buff it with Johnson floor wax. It would shine better than any hardwood floor ever would.

I went through things so I can teach others to be resourceful.

When I'm working with my clients, most of them are extremely limited income and other resources too. I tell them a lot about my past. I live in the better home now, I drive the better car, and I wear the better clothes. We want people to think we've always been that way and in order for me to work better with my clients, I have to get into a conversation with them and tell them about the home with the wood floor where I took bed sheets and made my first curtains and how I used to walk with cardboard as my shoe sole.

Sometimes when I'm working, it'll come to me, "How did you know that?" A lot of it I got from my mom and dad. My work ethics, I got from my dad because he was the hardest worker. My mom could take just nothing and make something out of it. I think the combination of him and her was put in me.

My advice to a woman in struggle is to first evaluate the situation. Then determine what you can do something about and what you can't, find out what, how and when you're going to do it, and get to work on it. You can't trash it, because it will hold you down.

I think everybody early in their lives hits a stagnated stage where you either go forward or backwards. When you're in that stage, you're looking at what to do with the rest of your life, how you're gonna pull from your past experiences.

The only way I knew how to live was to be directed by my belief and my faith and I got up and got my Bible. You know there is a difference in reading God's word and studying it and I went from reading to studying, then everything started falling in place. After studying it, I prayed, and I still label it as a stupid prayer. I warn people about stupid, ignorant prayer, that was my word, ignorant. My prayer was, "Lord, this is what I'm going to do, if this is what you want me to do, give me the strength to do it."

All these little things we say, "poor, poor me" about, would be "rich me, rich me" if we would get into a different view. "Poor me" is just a state of mind. I heard someone say once that we'll sit around and say, "poor me, poor me," until we start saying, "pour me another drink, pour me another drink." Sometimes we sit around and say, "poor me, sorry" until it's "pour me some more sorrow" and we don't want anything but sorrow. If I was to advise young women today how to sustain, I would tell them to push all the mess aside.

I wrote a lot of "Dear Jesus" letters because I had nobody else to tell and didn't want anybody else to know. I knew Jesus wouldn't tell anybody except what he wanted to intercede between me and God to plead my case. I would advise young ladies now that while you're down, going through problems, write it down. A lot of times, when you write things down, you'll find out things you really didn't know yourself and when you can read it again over and over, you can edit out the foolish stuff and concentrate on what's more important. Once you write it down, always have a pro and con – this is the good and this is the bad. What's good about this situation?

Now I know if I told someone that I found good out of my child dying, they would think I was crazy if they really didn't understand what I meant. But if I really, really, really believe that, if I hadn't lost that child, I would be probably, "poor me, poor me" until today. The death of that child put me in the position of seeing that I could have more and then that put me into going to college. I have impacted so many people's lives because of that one bad tragedy that happened in my life.

I would say to any young person that whatever the bad situation is, you take it and make it good.

One thing that helped me move forward in every bad situation is my faith in Christ. I remember the exact place I was, the children's bathroom. I was on my knees, I thought if I breathed, I would die, I was just that stressed. I remember the very moment when I just thought the words, "Lord help me." From that point on, I strengthened. It was as though I felt a hand on my shoulder and I got up. I've been up and down a lot of times since then, I've never been down where I couldn't at least think, "Lord help me." I think that was my turning point.

So I have a strong background with which to build my faith on. My dad is deceased now, my mom is still living and if they both go before me, if they left nothing else, they left faith that I have been able to pass on to my kids and grandkids. I know that's what has sustained me till I could go further.

Mae Hawkins

When I think about being powerless, I always reflect back to this one situation where I felt helpless. I think that's what led me to choose this career that I'm in. In 1981, my father became seriously ill. It happened all of a sudden. Just one hot day he was just walking through the pathway to his brother's house. It was real, real hot outside, and he had a heat stroke. They'd found him in the pathway between his home and his brother's house when I got the call saying they'd taken him to the hospital.

At the time I was transitioning from high school to college and I was back home because I had had my son. When I got to the hospital in Pine Bluff to see the results of what that stroke had done to him, I just felt powerless. It was like I couldn't help him. My father was lying there in a vegetative state like a baby. He was in a ball and it was very confusing. It happened all of a sudden with no warning. Usually when older people get sick you get a little warning. They can be sick one day and gradually get worse, but this happened all of a sudden. The process just sorta took its course by gradually getting worse and worse until we had to put him in a nursing home.

The transition that eventually made me so powerless was between the hospital and the nursing home when he couldn't feed himself. I had to work and my mom didn't have the transportation to get there to feed him like she wanted. She had kids, like my son - she babysat him. On my lunch break, I would go to the hospital to see him every day. The nurses would tell me - I was not a nurse then - "Oh, he can eat. We don't know what's wrong with him; he won't eat." I said, "He won't eat anything?" "No."

I would go talk to him. He couldn't respond at the time, but I was always told that they may not be able to talk to you but they can hear and be alert. So I would warn him,

> ## "Now dad, you have to eat to get stronger.
> ### They'll put a feeding tube in if you don't eat."

I was taking the nurse's word in the beginning. Then I thought, "When I'm here, he'll eat for me so maybe I need to come every day." So when I'd get there, some days it would be 1:00 p.m. and dinner was served at 12:00 p.m. I would go to his tray, which was pushed over in the corner, and he was lying in his bed, eyes open. I asked, "You hungry?" He'd make a nod like, yes, he was.

I would go to his tray. They'd told me on several occasions that he wouldn't eat. The fork was still in the plastic container and the hood looked like it had never been raised. All the food was still on the tray as if it had just been prepared. I was like, "Hmmm... is it that they don't have time and are not taking the time to actually feed him?" Granted, he could be slow and it would take probably an hour just to feed him properly. Or did he really tell them he wasn't hungry?

I don't know how I came to that conclusion, but my assumption was no attempt was ever made. He was in there for almost a month and that went on and on. At lunchtime, I made sure he ate. I would not even eat lunch. I'd go to the hospital and feed him. In the evening when I got off work, I rushed back and stayed there for supper so I knew he'd eat those two meals. He was real slow. It took me two hours sometimes to feed him.

Then I thought, "They're not taking care of him this way. Let me look at his hidey, 'cause you know you can get bed sores if you're not turned regularly." When I looked at his backside he had this great big old red area that had drainage coming from it; the odor was so bad. At the time, I didn't know; I wasn't a nurse. I was like, was this already on him? You know you never look at your dad there. Anyway, I felt at this stage it all boiled down to the poor care he was receiving. I don't know if it was because the family members were not there all the time. I don't know if it was because they didn't understand him or even attempt to take care of him.

I left the hospital one day in tears. I was just saying, "Oh my daddy is not going to get well; he's sick." And I just felt helpless like there was nothing I could do. I didn't know enough about medicine to know what they weren't doing.

Then one day I was in Dumas, on my lunch break. This girl had a flier that she had picked up that said something about Licensed Practical Nurse school testing was going on at Pine Bluff Tech in Pine Bluff.

I said, "LPN training, hmmm, that's a nurse and I don't wanna be no nurse. I ain't never wanted to be a nurse; my goal is to work with computers." That was when computers first started coming out and I was really interested. Then I thought, "A nurse, I think I'd make a good nurse." I talked to another girl, "Where is that test taking place?" She told me and said, "Let's me and you go." And I said, "OK, we'll do that." Then she said, "Naw, I don't wanna do that." I said, "Wait girl, you talked me into it. We're going and take this test."

So we went to Pine Bluff to take the test and let me tell you, it was so hard. There were a hundred plus people up there to take the test. At that time, the line was so long to get into nursing school. They said, "This first test, we're gonna weed out some of them and the first 60 that pass this test, we're gonna give them a second test." I thought, "Oh my gosh, I know I'm gonna be out of it."

They called me on the phone and said I was chosen in the first 60. I asked, "Out of a hundred plus people?" She said, "Yes, come in on Monday night and take the second one." I thought, "I probably won't get through the second one." So then I was called and told I was chosen in the 30 selected for the class. I said, "Oh boy, the angels are watching over me." Anyway, I took the class. I went to LPN school, and when I got out I started working at Delta Memorial Hospital in Dumas. That was in 1982.

I really loved nursing. I kept my dress white and I was eager to go to work. When I would enter the building, that's where it goes from hopeless and powerless to now I have some power and I'm in control. I can make a difference and I'm gonna make a difference. Others might look at me and I hope that they can see some good that I'm doing. That may make them want to be a nurse one day. Back then with my dad, I just had such poor, poor thinking of what that nurse was doing, and I didn't want to be that type of nurse. I knew that there were some good nurses out there; I'd seen them.

So while I was at that hospital, anything that had to be done, I volunteered to do it. Anytime they needed somebody, I'd go. I just wanted to be the best I could be. When I moved away from Arkansas in 1985, I relocated in Mississippi. I went to work down there in a larger hospital. That training I received at Delta Memorial Hospital just started taking its place. Everyone was saying "WOW, you're such a good nurse, you can do that? You know how to do this?" And I'd say, "Yeah." I'd tell everybody, "Start out first at a small hospital 'cause you get your most experience there."

I was charge nurse. I went to Registered Nurse school, don't let me leave that out, and received my Associate degree, and that's when I became a charge nurse on the 3 to 11 p.m. shift in the oncology unit at a hospital. Then my powerless feeling caught back up again.

When my patients would actually come in, they would be like you and me, healthy people, laughing and talking. Then they would get the diagnosis that they had some form of cancer. When I first saw them in such a healthy state, like I'm looking at you, I know… you're healthy now. I guess the stress in my face and eyes showed as I watched them deteriorate.

I'll never forget one Christmas Eve and we had this young boy. He was seventeen years old. We had followed him ever since he was twelve. His cancer got worse and worse. He had this girlfriend and he said he wanted to marry her. He was in high school. The situation was so sad and I had to be strong. I was the charge nurse coming in trying to make him feel comfortable, but it's hard to separate the two when your feelings, you know, get in there, and you're just like family.

He called me, pushed the button one day and said, "Would you ask Nurse Hawkins to come in, please?" I went in. He wanted me to just sit down and listen and talk to him. That's why I hate that nursing has kinda gotten away from that because we don't have time to really listen and talk 'cause we're so busy. I sat in there and talked to him. He said he wanted to marry this girl. My thinking was, "We don't know if you're gonna make it through tonight." His family didn't want him to marry the girl. He asked my opinion, and I tried not to give an opinion. I felt like that was a decision he needed to make.

I said, "No, let me just listen and hear both sides." Then I gave the pros and cons of what I thought of both sides. That night, he said he was marrying her tomorrow. That was the day before Christmas Eve. The pastor came and they bought the license. Everybody got prepared and they had a little bedside wedding. All the nurses on the unit were there.

He died Christmas Eve.

And oh, it just drained me so. It just took everything out of me because I had gotten too close, very much. I just felt like, Lord, I tried to be the best nurse I could be and there's still situations that I can't help. But then after I turned that around, I thought about it; I might have made a difference just by being there listening. I mean the illness was out of my control. I couldn't do anything for that but just be there and listen. I don't know how I might have touched him. He asked for me personally and that was touching too.

So, I could go on and on with experiences where I felt like I was powerless, but overall when I sit down and actually look at it, maybe I wasn't as power-less as I thought. Going back to my Dad's situation, I felt like the powerless-ness that I had there helped me grow to be the nurse that I am today. The situation with this young teenager who was dying with cancer, I feel like, me helping and being a part of his life and he also a part of my life helped me to grow and see things. Really, I look at it as we helped each other in both of my situations when I thought everything was out of control or I didn't have any control.

My son just graduated from college. One thing I asked him was, "What are some things you are good at?" Identify your strengths first and usually you can attach on to your strengths and you can exceed further. What do you like doing? Do you like drawing, reading, exercising? Once you know what your likes are, you can look at things in that area that may help you choose a career or focus on. I find that if you like doing it, you'll succeed at it more than something you dislike, or you're doing because someone told you. I find that to be very important.

I would like to add something, and this goes for anybody, old, young, black or white. I think you need to really sit back and find your inner person. Just think, what can I do, what was my purpose for being here on earth? I mean really seriously think about it. Write down on paper five purposes that you're fulfilling here on earth. If you were gone tomorrow, would anybody miss you? What accomplishments have you done so far on earth?

I feel like the Lord made all of us unique and different for a reason, and everybody has a purpose here on earth. All of it is not always bad. It should be something somebody else can say, once we're dead and gone, that we touched a life or made a difference in this area or something. And if you have not found that peace in your mind, that you made a difference, because I feel that everybody is unique in her own way, then maybe sit back and think things over. How can I make a difference? I think that's very important. I do that for myself. I came back to this community for a reason, because I could be living anywhere. I came back in 1990 and started work here. I've been offered all kinds of jobs with all kinds of salaries. I don't know why I just feel like I want to give something back to this community. Just research things and try to make a positive difference in someone's life.

Anna Huff

When I was growing up, I lived out in the country in a place called Jones Ridge. There was always a lot of activity and people, although we didn't have a lot of material things. We had each other and we had a sense of family; we had a sense of community.

When I was a child, we lived on a farm. My mom, my cousins, my sisters and brothers and I picked cotton after we got out of school and we'd quit a little bit before 5:00 p.m. There were eight of us children in my family and I was the fifth one. It's kinda like two sets of us. When the older ones finished high school, they left home. That left my sister over my younger sister, two brothers, and me. When I was fifteen or sixteen, I had to basically take over and run the household because my sister older than me got married and left. That left me being the oldest so I had to take care of all the financial responsibilities, pay the bills, buy the groceries because my mom would be sick so often. I became an adult at that time.

My mom didn't tell me, "You have to go to college or you need an education," but I saw how people treated her because she only had a seventh grade education. I saw how people talked to her, how she had to endure all of this stuff from social services and from people in general, it made me sick on the stomach. The furniture company would send out their collector to our house and he would say, "Is Bertha here?" I would just look 'cause she was three times the age of this person that was coming out. To me, education was the way to get out of the mold that everyone I loved and cherished seemed to be placed in because they were uneducated.

I just couldn't understand why it was so tangled up to me because in the black community you called your elders "Mr. and Mrs." White people didn't do that to black people but black people had to do that for white people and in my mind as a child that was very confusing. I felt that people of color were being treated as less of a person than the majority. Those people of color were my people and my relatives and I thought that they were just as important as anybody else in the world, to me they were my world. And for somebody to signify or denote that they weren't important, I took offense.

I guess that's when I became somewhat of a rebel.

I never missed a day of school, my mom didn't allow us to miss and we didn't want to miss. When I was growing up I went to Turner Elementary in the first grade.Everybody went to the same school and we were in an all black school. Then I started second grade and I was bused to Marvell, which was strange to me because I was used to going to this school in Turner where I knew people and the school was not far from home.

In fifth grade in 1970, schools were integrated. That was the first time that I ever encountered a white child in my class. At that point, I began to realize this black and white thing. And this black and white thing has not gone away. I could see how people treated them differently than they treated us. I don't know if it was because they had a little fear about if they did certain things, certain things might happen, I don't know what it was but it was so different.

I was a teenage parent and you know, there's so many disadvantages that go with that. First of all, I was so disappointed that I became a teenage parent but I knew it was my fault because I knew what not to do in order to not have a baby. A lot of girls know they shouldn't have babies but because I had the baby, do you treat me like I'm sub-human? Prior to having a baby, I had already decided, it can't be that you don't do the things that you had to do because you've had this baby.

During my high school years I was always a talented academic student so I graduated third in my class. When I got pregnant I didn't drop out of school. I came back, made the honor roll and made the same grades I made prior to having this child even though I was that child's primary care taker.

We all graduated high school. I was the first to go to college because I knew I had to go just for me and my sisters and brothers and my mother. I went to the University of Arkansas at Pine Bluff, majored in Business Administration and graduated in 1981.

When I graduated from college I had plans of moving to some big city and being some big executive. I ended up back in Marvell, did a lot of substitute teaching for the Marvell public schools, realized that was not my calling. I was going back and forth to Little Rock trying to find a job. I filled out the application at Boys, Girls, Adults Community Development Center in Marvell and I started working there in 1984 when I was about twenty-three.

BGACDC has always been a youth oriented organization. So programs were instituted to benefit children and families. Therefore, where were the youth? They're in the schools so there has to be a connection. Somewhere along the line the school and community, the parents and those entities had to work together. We were trying to figure out the most effective way to do this and BGACDC began to approach the schools.

BGACDC made a concerted effort and a decision that it was time that a female sat on the Marvell district school board and that it would be somebody who would represent the African American community. What BGACDC wanted, a large part of the community wanted, was to see things at a more even keel, to see all children have the opportunity for an equal education and a good education and that was not happening.

I ran for school board in 1988 when I was twenty-seven. I was being prepared or groomed to be that person who would hopefully sit in one of those seats and would represent a population. The intent was that it would be someone who would do some critical thinking, had participated in some leadership training, and also had exposure to things that would impact decisions to change the system. When I ran, there could be a majority African Americans with me being the first woman of color to be elected since the school integrated in 1970.

Not only was I on the ballot, there was a whole group of people who were on that ballot. Those were other single parents, black and white, the have-nots, people who had been left out of the main stream and the decision-making process. Those were the people that we, at BGACDC, worked with and for. It was really about so much more than just the school board election.

During that election, I felt that a lot of people who were opposed to my being there tried to tear a lot of that down. Their way of doing that was to belittle who I was and to try to come up with these judgments of who she is, what she's done and sort of judge me, hold me up to this light to say, she's not worthy.

The experiences were traumatic to say the least. There were attacks on me as an individual, there were attacks on my children, verbal attacks, never were we physically threatened. There were things said that I felt should not have been said about me. Never were those things said to me but people in the African American community were saying these things as well.

In the community, you find that if you don't own your home or own resources you're not seen as a leader by certain people. Therefore, during this whole campaign, to some people I wasn't seen as a person who was qualified. I didn't own anything, didn't own a car. So who was I to be in a position to make policy for a school district?

Although slavery is far-gone you still have people who are afraid of white people. You have black people who live on white people's property, who work for them, who basically depend on them for their livelihood. What was I asking people to do when I asked them to vote for me? That was a significant question. Am I asking you to jeopardize your life, your home, or your family? Are these things that you're willing to put out on a limb to support someone that you do believe in? You're not sure that she's gonna deliver because you don't know if she can, and if she can, will she be given the opportunity to deliver? Those were all issues that were very real.

115

I was an unwed mother. That was just totally against the grain. How could I think that I could be a school board member and I had this child when I was a teenager? I was sixteen when I had my son, I was fifteen when I got pregnant. I didn't see where it had anything to do with the election. I was a parent in a district of registered voters which is the only requirement that dictates who can serve on the school board.

I guess the most devastating thing to me about the whole campaign was when I heard that this African American educator had made the comments about me at the local pharmacy. That was a convening place for a lot of people of color because that was where you got your medication. She made a comment about being a single parent.

She didn't know if I should hold the office because of who I was.

She said to a white group of individuals, "She's not qualified." And I knew what this person said, because it was coming out of this person's mouth, it would be listened to by a lot of people. I really cried about that because I didn't know how to handle it at that point. I went to Beatrice, Executive Director of BGACDC, and told her that maybe it wasn't a good idea for me to run.

It just tore my heart to pieces because this was a person that I respected, who I thought would be a supporter. For those comments to come out of her mouth in that setting, I can't even put it into words. It impacted me more than probably a death of someone in my family because she literally killed me with those words.

During the first campaign I was elected, then served a five-year term and decided to run again. Prior to deciding to run again, my thought was to not run because of all the backlash and negative things that were done during the first campaign. The only thing that made me decide to stay in the race was my oldest son. I came home one day and I was so upset about it, he asked me what was going on and I tried to explain it to him. At that time he was nine years old.

I told him I was thinking about dropping out of the race, and he said, "No you're not, you've gotta run; you can't drop out, you can't quit!" At this point it became the whole concept of completing something that I had started. For him to see this thing run its full course was important for him and his friends. The young people were paying attention and this work was not finished.

I won the school board election, was a member for ten years and chair for six years.

In June of 2003 I had been experiencing some chest pains for about two or three months on and off. It would get to a point where I was so uncomfortable at night I couldn't sleep. The last episode before I ended up in the hospital, was one night, I attempted to lie in bed, my chest was hurting so bad I had to basically prop myself up and eventually sit up and the pain got so excruciating I started to cry. I told my significant other, Greg, about the pain and he asked if I thought I could make it through the night. I wasn't sure, as a matter of fact, I didn't sleep at all that night.

The next morning, we got up going to the Marvell medical clinic. There, the nurse practitioner examined me and said something wasn't right but she couldn't figure out what it was. So I told her all my symptoms and she said for me to go to my primary care physician and get an X-ray. I went to my physician, they did the X-ray and I knew something was wrong because everything became chaos in the doctor's office. He rushed me back into the office and told me that he needed me to go to the hospital.

I said, "What's going on?" He brought his other two partnering physicians in and had them to listen to my heart and they all had expressions on their faces that alarmed me. At that point he said, "I need you to go to the hospital right away, when can you go?" I said, "Well when do I need to go?" He said, "I need you to go right away. I need you to look at something." He showed me the X-ray and there was this mass in my chest and they thought it was attached to my heart so he thought I was about to have a heart attack.

We came back to the house, packed a couple of things and went to Little Rock. When I got to Little Rock, it was just as chaotic. They were waiting on me when I got there. I was sent to the heart hospital. I was under the pretense that I was about to have heart surgery because everybody was just crazy. I was checked into a room, whisked off to take some tests, this was like late afternoon. I had an ultra-sound at 2 a.m. The heart specialist came in and told me that it wasn't my heart and he was referring me to an oncologist.

The oncologist came in the next morning and told me that there was a mass about the size of both my fists. They did the biopsy and found out that it was malignant. I was diagnosed with non-Hodgkin's large cell lymphoma, which is a form of cancer of the lymph nodes. I met Dr. Millicent, now my oncologist. He told me that he was going to look into a treatment that would entail chemotherapy and radiation and he would like for me to start immediately.

I started out feeling a great sense of how little power I had. But then through this whole experience I really enhanced my sense of power over my body and over determining what happens to my body. I just want to share with people how important it is to have a sense of faith, a sense of believing in something that's greater than we are, I am.

My family was in and out of the hospital including my sister-in-law who is a very spiritual person who had come to my rescue and was counseling and praying. My minister was there, my sister, my children, it was just phenomenal the outpouring of support and love that surrounded me from that point on. I knew that I had nothing to worry about. I had control of this even though I didn't know the medicine or what they might have to do. I made a decision,

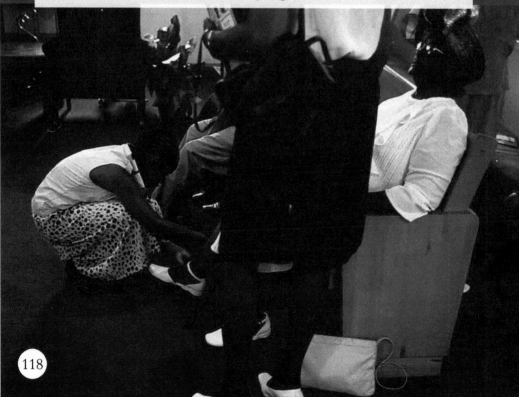

I'm going to stand steadfast on my faith and I know that I will be healed.

The pastor of my church who lives thirty-five minutes from Marvell would come by my house every Tuesday before I went for chemo on Wednesday. We would have prayer and read scriptures. He sent scriptures from the Bible for me to read every week. When I went to chemo in Little Rock he was there for each treatment. From day one, this man began a process of meeting with me, sharing the word, the Bible with me, providing me with daily readings, coming by to have prayer with me, singing songs with me and developing the sense of easiness, of not having to be afraid or worry about what was gonna happen.

I was so concerned about how my daughter was going to react when she finally realized what was going on. I said to her, "You say you believe in God and we know, based on what He's done before, that He heals and He has the power to do anything that we want Him to do, all we have to do is ask and believe that He'll do it." And she said, "Well yeah, you know I believe in God."

I said, "If you believe in God, pray for the healing and leave it alone, don't dwell on it." She said, "Well, that's easy to say, I don't understand how you can sit there and say that." I told her, "I prayed about it and I read His word, and it's been reconfirmed to me that He is who He says He is, He's everything and if you need something, ask Him for it. And so I'm standing on that and I believe in that."

During this time one thing I was really trying to figure out was how I was going to deal with losing my hair. My sister said, "Well, I have a solution. I'm gonna send you something, and when you get it, call me." The package came, I opened the box and there were thirty-one scarves in the box, also a mannequin's head with a scarf tied on it showing me how to tie the scarf. I have never been one who was creative as far as sewing and baking and she's aware of that. She gave me a model to go by. When I went to work I would have my scarf on, and I am very fashionable, so my scarves would always match my attire.

I lived about one and a half hours from Little Rock where I went for chemotherapy and radiation. Friends helped me drive and sometimes I drove myself. All of my chemo treatments were intravenously induced which means the fluids were put into me and there's just so much your body can hold and you will have to go to the bathroom. There's few bathrooms between Little Rock and Marvell.

On one occasion in late July I had to use the bathroom so bad. It was so hot and the mosquitoes were so bad. It was dusk dark and we had gotten on this long stretch where we knew there was no place to go use the bathroom. We pulled over into literally a field. My sister stood behind me and her friend stood in front of me and I was on the side of the car trying to squat and my sister almost knocked me in the ditch. I was so tired and so weak that I could barely make it but we all laughed and cried so hard because the mosquitoes were tearing my rear end up and then she almost knocked me over into the weeds!

Through this whole experience not only did I learn the power of support and the power of prayer and faith, my daughter learned, my siblings learned, people outside of my family learned. The people even outside of my immediate community, Little Rock, Michigan, from everywhere would call and we'd have prayer on the phone. I couldn't believe the flowers I got. It was just amazing, such an out-pouring of love. It gave me a strength that I never knew I had.

The first time I went to the doctor after beginning chemo treatment the tumor had been reduced by fifty percent, the second time it was seventy-five percent. The physician would say, "This is just amazing." I would say, "Yeah, it's amazing to you, but I know what's going on." My minister came the night before my fourth round of chemo and he said, "The time is right." I said, "What are you talking about?" He said, "It's time for man to lay hands on you." That's something that we do in a healing process, whereby the person who has supposedly the power to heal lays hands on you and the healing takes place.

He said, "The Lord told me that the time is now." So he read a scripture in the Bible, had me to place my hand over the spot where the tumor was located and he placed his hand on my hand and started to pray. I could just feel, I don't know how to describe it, I could feel this power coming from him to me. After he finished, he told me, "Now when you go tomorrow, they won't find a sign of this tumor."

So the next day I went in and I took the X-ray. Dr. Millicent is this happy go lucky guy and also spiritual which was really a support to me as well, we'd always talk about something in the Bible. He came in and told me I looked good. It was Greg and I and my minister who would always meet me in Little Rock on my chemo days. My minister was sitting outside and he had told me the night before, "Now when the doctor tells you that he can't find anything, don't say a word, don't tell me anything, I don't wanna know."

So when Dr. Millicent came in, I asked, "Did you look at my X-ray?" He said, "No, I didn't, let me go take a look at it." So he went out and he came

back and said, "Come here, I need you to look at something." The X-ray was hanging out in the hall where the nurse's station is located and they were all looking at it when I got there. He had two pictures, one he had taken when I first came in which had the mass protruding from under my rib cage and then he had another picture. He said, "You remember when you took this one?" I said, "Yes." He said, "Well look at this one and tell me what you see." I looked and I looked and I told him, "There's nothing there!" He said, "You're right, there's nothing there. You look just as healthy as anyone else that I have seen who has never had cancer."

My pastor just looked at me and smiled and didn't say a word. From that point on, I know that anything that I have to deal with, I have no doubt about it, I know that I can conquer anything. You just have to have faith.

I went to the doctor yesterday and he's just still in awe because I'm doing wonderful, there's no sign of any kind. Everything is just perfect. That's the word he used, he said, "You look perfect to me. You look perfect on the in-side and perfect on the outside." I have to go back in three months. I started out going every three weeks then it moved to six weeks, eight weeks and now it's six months.

The women in my church who are my third cousins, are now in their eighties. Those women, when I was a child, were the ones who made sure you did what you suppose to do, made sure you didn't do what you weren't suppose to do and gave me that base of my spiritual being. Because, I don't think that a lot of things that I have encountered and that I've achieved would've hap-pened if I had not had a spiritual belief and believed in a higher power. My church, which was a country church, was very important to me.

As I got older, I made a conscious decision that I was going to be a part of the solution and not a part of the problem. That's why my hand is in some places where it probably shouldn't be. I don't want to be one of those folks who sit back and say, "They should have done that," or "Why are they doing this?" I want to be one of the folks who actually is a part of the doing. I may not always be a part of the doing, but be a part of the conversation in regards to what should be done.

I tell any girl today to be wise, make smart decisions and don't have a child until you're ready financially, emotionally, until you're ready to be a parent because I was not ready to be a parent.

I take that so seriously because that advice could either make or break a young person's life. One thing that I would definitely tell them is that they must be true to themselves. They've got to realize that whatever decision they make, they have to live with it. Also, it has to be one that I feel is right for me not one that I feel a decision someone else wants me to make, one that's truly right for me.

When you're trying to do something it's just so important that you have a reliable support base. Beatrice, Executive Director of BGACDC, keeps saying certain people that worked at the Center would have made it anyway without the Center. I totally disagree. If nobody else was in my corner, I knew she was in my corner. If she was in my corner, I knew that two other co-workers were in my corner because we just had a relationship like that. It was more than colleagues. It was more about family and taking care of each other and taking care of each other's family.

There's so many women here that don't think they have a way out. They think they have to rely on a man to take care of them. I keep telling them, "You can do this for yourself, you just have to make the first step and once you make that first step, that's the hardest thing to do. Try! Try!"

Anita Harrison

When I had my first child at age nineteen, I was with his father. There was a lot of abuse in the relationship – physical, emotional, it was like being trapped inside of a well that a woman couldn't get out of. Family members were there for me but I didn't want them to get involved, I didn't want them to get hurt nor myself. It felt almost like being by yourself. When I had the second one we were still together at the time, threatened one miscarriage by him pushing me down on my stomach. It was a struggle to sit there day after day trying to keep your head up. Older people kept telling me to keep my head up 'cause one day it was gonna get better. We were together for maybe nine and a half years and it was mostly physical, emotional and verbal abuse.

We met through a cousin of mine who was going with his best friend in 1989. I was getting ready to graduate from high school. She like, "He's a good guy, he's this, he's that." Of course he started out being a good guy until actually I got out on my own and I found out exactly how he was.

His personality at the time was a good aspect. He carried himself in a way that would trick a person easily, because he talked and all of that. He was more experienced of being out there in the world, so that was kinda an attraction to me. Our names began with the same letter, I just thought it was it.

I was living in Postelle, Arkansas outside of Marvell, with my grandparents. Of course my grandmother and my grandfather was telling me, "You need to get your education, don't be bothered about that one man 'cause he is this, he that." They were trying to get me not to get too involved with him because he was going to be a bad influence. His dad was the same way and if the dad is like that nine times out of ten the son's gonna be like the daddy because they see the daddy doing it to they momma and stuff like that.

But being seventeen you think you know it all.

After I graduated from high school I stayed around the house mostly helping my grandmother out, doing cleaning and stuff like that. She was telling me, "You done went and got yourself pregnant." And I kept telling her I wasn't pregnant. She said I was pregnant because I was sleeping more than I normally sleep. I went to the doctor and sure enough she was right. She was telling me, "I ain't goin' do nothing for you. Don't even ask me to buy the baby Pampers." And she was the first one who bought the Pampers and clothes. He couldn't sleep with me, I couldn't bathe him, I couldn't do nothing.

It was sort of uneasy and scary all at the same time, being a single mom, but I did have a lot of help, 'cause my mother was still living at the time. I had an older sister that had three or four children. So that was some more experience right there, and I used to keep hers and my auntie's children too, so I knew a little bit about taking care of a baby, but not as much as I would like to have known before I had him. I finally decided to venture out on my own. I was twenty at the time.

My boyfriend, I did write him and let him know I was pregnant. Of course, he was locked up down there in Helena jail. Disorderly conduct, fighting, or something. He was in jail and they let him know I had had his child and he was happy. His mother named him. It ended up being a good thing because when he got out, he came right on and picked him up. Then he dropped outta the picture again 'cause I left and went to Texas with my brother.

I went to Texas in 1992. Charvez, my son, was going on a year old then. My mom died in February of that year and so I just packed up everything we had and went up there with them, my brother and his wife. I stayed up there for about a month and a half and I told him I wanted to come home, I missed the country life. Everything. I couldn't go fishing, couldn't dip my snuff 'cause she don't want dipping, smoking, none of that in her house. "I know y'all got to take me back to Arkansas. And when I got back to Arkansas that was the first thing I did was got me a dip and went on the fish creek.

When I came home, my boyfriend was in the hospital because he had got beat up, some boys had jumped him or something. When he got out he came and seen Charvez, thought we was goin back together, but I told him, "Naw, I don't think so." Long about that time I found out I was pregnant with the second child. I started out in college but I had to drop out because it was kinda hard walking up and down the stairs carrying books.

They had just built the Manor apartments in Marvell so I went and filled out the application. It was close to my time when I moved up there in December and I had him in January. We started living together about three months after my second child was born.

The fighting started in '93. The first time, I was pregnant with his second child by me. Everybody that came around, he thought I was sleeping with or they wanted to sleep with me. I couldn't talk to a man unless I was messing with that man. He just went flying all off the handle. He actually punched me in my stomach, 'cause he was telling me that I was pregnant and it wasn't none of his. I went to the hospital because I started bleeding. They stopped it and everything was okay. I came home, he said the same thing. He was goin' do this and do that, always saying he was goin' straighten up. Each time that I threatened a miscarriage, the doctors did something to keep me from having a miscarriage. I was too far along, like maybe seven or eight months.

Each time his momma come over, she talked to him and tell him, "You wrong. If she has you arrested, you goin' say she did you wrong. If she get

up the nerve to do something to you in your sleep, you think your family is goin' be mad at her. But they ain't goin' be mad at her because you ain't got no business treating her like that. Because that's a good woman and she needs to be respected and treated like a good woman."

"I ain't gonna do it no more Momma, I promise."
That's what he's telling his momma.

When he would beat me up the children was present. My oldest would get so mad, he'd ball his fist up and sit up in a corner. At night when my boyfriend went to sleep, he would wake up and actually find the son that looked like him and the son next to the oldest standing up over him staring at him. I think that kinda got to him because the boys are protective of their mother. The one that look just like him is just like him, hateful, you can never tell what he goin' do.

They always knew that he wasn't gonna go too far. He knew how far to go. He would punch and that's it. He wasn't goin' do nothing else, punch one time and then go on about his business. He got his frustration off or whatever.

The last time we got to fighting was in 1999 when he hit me with a gas pipe that go on a stove. He cut the cord of the refrigerator so the food would spoil. I told him, "Your kids need something to eat." He said, "Get it the best way you can."

When I did get out of it in 1999, it was the best choice I made. It was hard but it was good because it taught me to keep my head held high and never to let anyone break my spirit. I was by myself up town, two years, maybe longer. It was like I was attracting the wrong type of men. So I thought, I'm just gonna' be myself and I started being myself – quiet, relaxing, stay at home kinda gal, straight out country girl. Their daddy was more like a city slicker and I wasn't.

Last year, 2005, about this time, me and my sister and brother-in-law had went fishing and I was just still sitting around my house. We went to the store and I seen him (my new boyfriend). We had talked a long time ago but by me being in that situation I was in, he backed off. He didn't want me to get hurt. This particular day we was at the store, he was pumping his gas and I was going in the store so he waved and I waved, I didn't think nothing else of it.

'Bout 7:00 p.m. that night I heard a car pull up then a knock on my door. I said, "Who's this knocking at my door at this time of the night?" I was trying to cook the kids something to eat. I opened the door and looked and said, "Didn't I just see you at the store?" He said, "Uh-huh. It was something that my mind wouldn't let me rest. I went home but my mind just wouldn't let me rest. Something just kept telling me, I needed to come back up here where you was at and find you." He asked everybody where I stayed, because everybody up town knew me, 'til he found my house.

Well that country boy found that country girl and it was just a connection. Ever since then we been talking and getting along fine. We don't have no problems I guess cause we way out here. We don't have no company.

He helped me to get out of it too, because everybody else that I was talking to, they was scared of my old boyfriend. But this particular one showed him that he wasn't scared of 'em. He told him, "I'm over here with her and that's

how it's gonna be. You're out, you had her, you didn't treat her right, so I'm fixing to show you how she suppose to be treated." My old boyfriend didn't like that, he didn't like that at all. So he showed him that he was goin' come up and hit me. He got mad and swung at me, the guy caught his hand and beat him up. From then on I ain't had no problems outta him.

I told him, "Now, if I knowed what I knew now, you'd be dead. Before you think ever of putting your hands on me again, I ain't your woman, I ain't your wife. 'Cause now, with the attitude I got, baby I'll stab you." He said, "You wouldn't do that to me." I said, "Oh yes I would. You ain't taking nothing of mine. If it's on me or in my house you ain't taking it. I refuse to give up something that's mine."

So he started telling folks I was crazy. I said, "I sho is crazy. Mess with me now, I'll show you how crazy I am 'cause right now, I am crazy, 'cause what you put me through." I learned from it and I learned what to hurt a man is. "Now you wanna try me?" He said, "No, I'm fixing to go." Actually we get along better now that we ain't together than we did when we was together.

My fiancé, when he comes in, he hugs and kiss me on my check and says to the boys, "That's how you treat a woman." When he leaves, that's what he do. He and I both tell them, "If you want respect, you got to give respect especially when it comes to a woman. You don't want a woman to always cook, clean, wash your clothes. Get in there and help your mama do it so you can learn how to do it. Your mama is teaching you how to be a man. Therefore, you don't have to worry about putting your hands on no woman 'cause you get mad 'cause she won't do something for you."

Now the one that's just like his daddy, it's goin' take a little bit more help with him. He done started out already 'cause I have to get on him all the time about his little stepsister. I tell him, "You do not hit girls, that is so ugly." He says, "Well mama, she hit me." I say, "That still ain't no reason for you to hit her. If she hits you, come and tell me, that's what I am here for." It's slowly sinking in to him.

We moved into this house in October of last year, 2004. I just planted me a garden today too, a sketch of a garden, 'cause I was goin' put it behind the house and I asked the man who farm this land not to put beans [soybeans] that close to the house but he did it anyway. So I had to get me a shovel and go there while digging me some baits [worms], turned the dirt over and threw me some turnip greens out there.

Up close to the house I turned that over and put me some cucumber seeds out there. I got around this little hole and on one side, I got garlic, on the other side I got peas. I had some pots, I put some soil in the bottom, planted me some bell peppers and some cabbage. I said I'm gon' have me a garden one way or another. I got to do one more to make my tomatoes. I got to find me some mustard greens to go with the turnip greens, then I'll be through.

My old boyfriend came by Saturday, was talking to his children. I was hanging out some clothes, so I walked out there to see what he was talking about. He asked me if I was happy, I told him, "I am very happy with what I got now 'cause I ain't going through no physical, emotional, none of that kind of abuse, and the boys are treated like they some humans, whatever they want, they got, whatever I want, I got, so I ain't worried about nothing now. Don't you see me always smiling?" He said, "Yeah."

"All that should tell you something, you weren't doing something right."

He asked me if I ever was gon' get married. I told him "Yeah, I plan on getting married before I reach thirty-five." He said, "I hope it don't be nobody that I know." I said, "Who knows, it may be somebody you know but it ain't gon' be nobody nearly like you."

When I first left my grandmothers, I was always wanting to do something besides sit at home. It was like sit at home, go to my auntie's, sit at home, go to my auntie's. When Kerin (friend and community organizer in Marvell) came and asked me about Delta Women Achieving Goals (DWAG), I told her, "Yes, I'll come to a meeting." It sounded interesting and when I did get into it, reading about it, I said, "Now I'm getting somewhere, he ain't goin' to be able to hold me back now. If I can get in this I know I'll have enough strength and courage to walk away."

The more she talked to me about DWAG and doing these different things in Marvell, she didn't know at the time she was building up my confidence to leave him. I have to give her credit. Her getting me involved with DWAG build up my courage to leave him.

The more I went to those meetings and heard the old women talking, the better I felt. I said, "Oh yes, Lord, this is what I've been praying for, this is my miracle." So, yes, DWAG and BGACDC [Boys, Girls, Adults, Community Development Center] definitely helped me get out of that one.

Being with the women, listening to them, their strength, 'cause I knew that they came through some things back in them old days when my grandparents were coming up. I know them women had to be tough, I know I got to have some strength somewhere. The more I listened to them talk, the better I felt. The more I was seeing, it was one in particular, Ms. Chesa and she was telling me what she and her sister went through. I said, "Oh yeah, I can do this." That helped me.

The quiet Anita wanted to be controlled, 'cause that's where I was with him. I said, "Lord, there's something I'm not doing right, I just don't know what I'm doing wrong." Because they can't say that I'm mean or hateful and that I'm this or that 'cause when I'm with somebody I be just that one person. It's got to be something... and it came to me, be yourself, don't try to change to be somebody that you are not.

So that's what changed,
I stopped trying to change to be the people those men wanted me to be
and was being who I am.
The good 'ole country girl, that's what it was.

If I had that opportunity again, I would listen instead, 'cause it was hard. And now that I'm out of it, I tell my boys especially the two that I got by him, that's not how you treat a woman. Whatever you do, don't put your hands on a woman. I'll tell anyone, "Before you get involved in a relationship with a man, find out what he about."

I'd tell a young woman with a man like that, "Run and get out of it as quickly as you can. He did it once, he'll do it again." They always goin' put on a sad face. "I'm sorry, I ain't goin' do it no more." Don't listen. Listen to what your mind is telling you and get out, GET OUT. Run for the border.

So it was a blessing 'cause I learned a lot, how to be independent, very independent. He made me be independent 'cause I was doing everything for the boys by myself. If something came up broke, he was never there to fix it so I had to learn how to fix it. The guy that I'm with now, he always ask me, "Why you don't ever ask me for nothing?" I say, "The only time I need to ask you for something is if I can't get out and get it for myself, I am very independent." I was so use to doing stuff for myself and now that I got somebody that's helping, it's kinda hard, you know, to take that hand. I told him that's just the way I am, independent, very independent.

I don't ask my folks for nothing unless I have to. My auntie tells me all the time that I'm too independent, too much like my mother. I can't help it, I had to be 'cause they wouldn't give me nothing, they was scared that he was goin' take it. It's just the attitude, it's all about the attitude that I got now, a new look on life. That I can do anything I wanna do when I put my mind to it. I just recently, last month, went and enrolled at Phillips Community College. All I got to do now is go down and get my schedule. I start this fall.

The Community
Storytelling Project

In the 1980's while I worked as director of the Social Work Division at the Arkansas Department of Health, the agency began offering in-home nursing and social work care. Judy Chastain, my assistant and good friend, and I split the state in half and we each visited homes in our part of Arkansas. Sometimes Judy and I drove for hours to visit one home health patient in the mostly rural state.

After each visit as I drove back to Little Rock I remember thinking, "I wish I could document the struggles and strengths of these patients and share these stories with others in Arkansas. People would learn to live using their own courage, persistence and faith, just like the patients I came to know through this work."

I never documented this. However, as life sometimes goes, it gave me a second chance. In 1996 I began working with a group of women from eastern Arkansas, a region known as the Mississippi River Delta, or "the Delta." This book shares the stories and photos of ten wonderful African American women who carry with great dignity the courage, persistence and faith I saw ten years before with the patients at the Health Department. The resulting stories showcase the indomitable spirit of African American Delta women.

In the fall of 1996 Freeman McKindra, Senior Vice President of the Winthrop Rockefeller Foundation, Sister Mary Walz, Anna Huff and I stood talking after a planning meeting in Little Rock. We expressed concern about the coming welfare "reform" legislation. Many believed the legislation would

only hurt poor women in the Delta area of Arkansas where women did not work because no industry, very little commerce and almost no jobs existed in their small rural towns. They wanted to work; however, with the new reform they would lose the small stipends and health insurance through Medicaid that they currently had for their children.

In the conversation we talked about the possibility of St. Elizabeth's Health Center in Gould and Boys, Girls, Adult Community Development Center (BGACDC) in Marvell coming together to start a women's group to focus on creating small businesses for women in the two small rural communities in the Arkansas Delta. Each town had a population of around 1,500 residents. Both community based organizations worked with women who would be affected by this legislation.

Sister Mary Walz worked as the social worker at the health center operated by the Daughters of Charity in Gould. Before she

began working at the clinic she came to the Arkansas Delta to help conduct a needs assessment to determine whether this was an underserved area for health care. They identified the need for health services and St. Elizabeth's provided

both preventive and primary care to the residents of the area. In addition, the center served as a support system, organizing location, and second family for the residents, especially poor families in Gould.

Anna Huff, who grew up in Marvell, Arkansas, about twenty minutes east of the Mississippi River, worked as the resource development director and assistant to Beatrice Shelby, the director of BGACDC. Having lived all her life up to that point in Marvell and having been a single mother who survived for a while on welfare assistance, Anna clearly understood the struggle of poor women in the Delta, especially African American women. She as well

as anyone knew the terrifically hard time women without jobs would be facing soon. She felt a strong sense of responsibility and commitment to help create opportunities for self-sufficiency for women.

In January 1997, twenty-five women involved in programs or receiving services from St. Elizabeth's and BGACDC came together with Anna Huff, Sister Mary, and myself for the first meeting of what was to become

143

"DWAG" or Delta Women Achieving Goals. From the beginning everyone wanted to base the work on strengths and assets and not weaknesses or needs.

We met at least once a month for two years learning about the communities and small business development as well as ways that African American women could be involved in the decision making structure in their two towns.

After many discussions and visiting small businesses, the women decided to concentrate first on building their communities and organizing to be a part of this development. They were ready to collect information about their towns and become involved in change through collective work. They received funding for community organizing and community building from The Women's Foundation of Arkansas, Daughters of Charity, Ms Foundation for Women, and Catholic Campaign for Human Development.

The DWAG women were interested in learning about their communities, the issues of concern, and how they could contribute to building and improving their towns. For this work DWAG received funding from the United Methodist Church Women's Division, Social and Environmental Justice Office, to receive training and conduct a participatory rural appraisal (PRA) in Marvell and Gould. Pamela Sparr, program director in Washington, DC, secured this funding, found a facilitator to provide the training in Arkansas, and attended herself for the week.

Andrea Robles traveled from the University of Wisconsin Madison to teach for ten days the different tools we would use to collect information and then to analyze what we collected. In the end we would have a plan for action for each of the two communities. The plan would address a high priority issue of concern in each community.

One of the tools or activities led to the idea of the oral history project. Several of the younger women, nineteen to twenty-two years old, sat on one side facing several of the older women, thirty to sixty years of age. The younger ones interviewed the others about their lives. They had created a list of questions and took turns asking them. After the interviews, participants discussed the activity. The younger women loved the interviewing and hearing about the lives and stories of the older women. The struggles of the older women and how they overcame these life challenges fascinated them.

While the younger women struggled with life crises such as domestic violence, substance abuse and teen pregnancy they identified with the older women as role models and inspiration. After this PRA, DWAG members created Delta Youth Achieving Goals (DYAG). This high school group carried out the goals of the plan for youth and also participated with the women in community projects.

During the 1998 PRA, one of the activities involved learning how to interview. The person selected to be interviewed in Marvell was Marty (Robinson) McKissic. Marty worked at the time at BGACDC as the coordinator of the organization's oral history project. Soon after the PRA was completed, Marty became the DWAG/DYAG program coordinator for BGAC-DC.

At this point I talked with a friend, Rick Foster, Vice President of Rural Development and Agriculture at the W.K. Kellogg Foundation about the stories and he suggested I interview two of the women and send him stories. I interviewed Gertrude Jackson and Jean Davis in 1999 and 2000 and sent him edited ver-

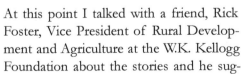

145

sions of the interviews. We submitted a proposal that he funded to conduct an oral history project in the two communities. We combined this funding with the dollars we had received from the other foundations and local donors to support two community organizers and a program coordinator.

From January of 2002 to the summer of 2003 community teams of high school students and women, DYAG and DWAG members, planned and documented, through oral history interviews, the lives of sixty-four African-American women between the ages of eighteen to one hundred-two in Marvell and Gould.

DWAG and DYAG members interviewed women they recognized as accomplishing a lot in spite of heavy odds, or women about whom they said, "We want to hear more, we want to hear their stories." They selected women from different generations and work histories who faced a variety of struggles in their lives. Sister Mary Walz, Anna Huff, Marty McKissic (DWAG and DYAG Project Coordinator) and I taught the members the process for conducting the project. Helen Lewis from the Highlander Center for Education and Research in New Market, Tennessee came to teach the members interviewing and recording processes. Marty McKissic and several DWAG members transcribed the tape-recorded interviews, and at a community reception the women received copies of their interviews.

The DWAG/DYAG members and team then selected ten women out of this group of sixty-four women to be highlighted in a book, a traveling photography exhibit and a children's piece.

Becky Williams interviewed the women between 2004 to 2007. They tell of the women's experiences during the years 1950 to 2004. The photographs were taken in 2004 (*Appendix 1*, Characteristics of the Women, *page 152; and Appendix 2*, Interviews of the Women, *page 153*).

As the author and editor of this book, in 2003 I began meeting with the ten women individually either at BGACDC or St. Elizabeth's Health Center and asked them to share about their life journey. Five of the women lived in Marvell and five lived in Gould.

Specifically, I asked each woman to share a life experience or crisis where she felt distressed, oppressed, hopeless or helpless; a second experience where she felt the competency and power to make decisions in her life and create more equity in her community; and what happened during her life that helped her change. Each woman chose the experiences from her life she wanted to share (*Appendix 3*, Experiences shared by the ten women, *page 154*).

At different ages when interviewed, the women talked about different years in their lives. The earliest experiences shared took place in the 1950's. The most recent experiences shared took place in 2004.

Laurent Guerin, a photojournalist, lived in the communities of Gould and Marvell during the summer of 2004 and photographed the women in their homes, daily routines, and in their communities. The color photos serve as a window into the daily activities of the individuals as well as the characteristics of the region including customs and traditions, food, work, recreation and community.

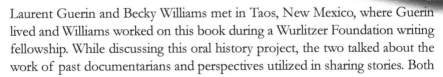

Laurent Guerin and Becky Williams met in Taos, New Mexico, where Guerin lived and Williams worked on this book during a Wurlitzer Foundation writing fellowship. While discussing this oral history project, the two talked about the work of past documentarians and perspectives utilized in sharing stories. Both

wanted to present the stories of the women's lives through lenses of dignity and integrity. The historical documentarian who came to mind was Lewis Hine, sociologist and photographer of early 1900's.

Dr. Kate Sampsell-Willmann, a leading Lewis Hine researcher stated, "I think that he (Lewis Hine) was in the right place at the right time, and a very good, decent human being, who had the ethic of recording data, instead of trying to force purely emotional, sort of, pathetic vision onto people… When he turned his camera on people, he didn't objectify them, didn't make them so they are objects in an argument. He subjectified them, made conversations with them, and preserved their dignity." *(Boyd, Taylor, "Interview with Dr. Kate Sampsell-Willmann",* Lewis Hine: A Crusader with A Camera. *Lewsihinehd.weebly.com)*

The work of collecting people's stories and recording these stories to share with others has a long history of promoting passing on traditions and ideas from generation to generation as well as promoting social justice.

One afternoon at a DWAG meeting at St. Elizabeth's Health Center, I asked the members whom they wanted to reach and influence with these stories. The members of DWAG/DYAG determined their target audience to be women and youth in the midst of struggle and those who came through the struggle and benefited from recognizing the power in themselves. They also believed that everyone concerned about how people can overcome barriers and find a sense of personal power would benefit from the women's stories.

The women's struggles continued over years. They did not solve these crises or inequalities overnight. Their actions sowed seeds to help others, especially African American women, create a more just society. They worked for the long haul by using a support group of family and friends that they trusted; meeting with a working group with regular meetings; attending church, praying and receiving support from their pastor; planning lots of times for food and celebration; looking at past experiences of older people and using these as inspiration; recognizing their personal values and taking action based on these; taking time for reflection and disengagement; and, viewing situations from an historical perspective and learning from the past. (*see Appendix 4,* Social justice issues and non-violent tactics employed, *page 153*).

Others can now use the example of the formation of Delta Women Achieving Goals and Delta Youth Achieving Goals and the process of using women's life stories and experiences as tools for change in organizing and moving people to action.

Acknowledgements

A great thanks to the communities of Marvell and Gould, Arkansas and all the members of Delta Women Achieving Goals and Delta Youth Achieving Goals. Special thanks to Marty McKissic, Anna Huff and Sister Mary Walz for your incredible work, love, and sharing your hospitality and a bed. Thanks to Marty McKissic and Donna Glover for transcription services without which this book would not exist and to Beatrice Shelby for constantly being available with support, advocacy and information.

All my love to my family support group, Amy and John Shadell, Gene Williams, Ann Williams, and all the Clark and Jeude family. Much love to my late parents, Helen and Gaylon Clark who through their support and funding I was able to parcel time to write this book over a period of twenty years, and a special thanks to my late dear brother David who taught me the true meaning of courage, persistence and faith. I wish to thank my good friends for their supportive good cheer: Leah Wilkinson, Kathryn Matchett, Becky Butler, Jean Speegle, Christie Kriebel, Tom Gallagher, Lisa Hoashi, Leah Matsui, Linda Hattendorf, Barbara Zaring, Rick Foster, Judy Chastain, and Marie Sandusky. To my friends and supporters whom I could not mention here by name, please know that I thank you from the bottom of my heart.

I am particularly indebted to my "teachers" - Paul Thomas, DePauw University, Chair, Sociology Department; Helen Lewis and Susan Williams, Highlander Research and Education Center; Don Rothman and Paul Skenezy, University of California Santa Cruz; Kent Wong, Director of the Labor Center at University of California Los Angeles; Gilda Haas, SAGE Popular Education Center; and Pamela Sparr, United Methodist Church Women's Division. Great thanks to John Kirk, University of Arkansas at Little Rock, Director, Anderson Institute on Race and Ethnicity, writer of great books on the history of the Delta and civil rights, and without whom I would not have reached the finish line. Thanks to Grif Stockley who introduced me to the history of the Delta and suggested that these stories could fill a void in written stories about African American women in this region.

A special shout out to my dear friends in Costa Rica: Julieta Mendez Rojas and family Mendez Rojas, Copa Buena; Juan Bautista Cruz, Libreria El Kiosko, San Vito; Rebecca Cole, Jardin Botanico; and the staff at Hotel Bougainvillea, Santo Tomas de Heredia.

Special thanks to three great mentors Freeman McKindra, Tom Bruce and Mary Dillard who taught me all about rural development, organizational development and how to run a business; much gratitude to my associates of

Becky Williams and Associates, Lewis Leslie, Chris Patterson and Lynnette Watts who served as cheerleaders and encouragers over the long haul. Best wishes for my young friend and videographer/film producer, Walt Peterson; special thanks to my dear friend Michael Knight, Wurlitzer Writing Fellowship, Taos, New Mexico who gave me the time to rest so I could write these stories

Much of the work for this book took place in a very cozy writing spot, River City Coffee in Little Rock, Arkansas. All my love, Jeremy Bragg and Regi Ott and my fellow coffee mates.

Thanks for the love and faith of my church buddies: Little Rock United Methodist Church members, UMW Sarah Circle, and Unity Sunday School Class.

A special shout out to my good friends of the Kellogg National Fellowship Program, Group 10 and our wonderful KNFP 10 Writing Group led by Don Rothman where seeds for this book were planted.

A special thanks to my new friend Kat Robinson who did the layout for this unique and beautiful book.

Appendix 1

Characteristics of the women selected for the book	
Things all women had in common	**Differences among the women**
Women with children	Women lived during different decades and generations
African American	Different kinds of work
Shared about their mothers	Different levels of education: from some high school to college degree
Lived in Marvell or Gould most of their lives	Some attended segregated schools, some integrated schools, and some both
All worked outside the home as an adult and were the main wage earner much of the time in their adults lives	Some grew up working and living on farms.
Went to public schools in the Delta	Number of children varied from one to ten
	Depending on the generation, some had no access to public family planning services and some had access
	Some grew up with no electricity or indoor plumbing, some had these

Appendix 2

Interviewers and Dates			
Name	**Interviewer/s**	**Locations**	**Dates**
Gertrude Jackson	Becky Williams	BGACDC and at home	May 18, 2001 May 25, 2001 Aug. 7, 2007
Jean Davis	Becky Williams	BGACDC and at home	Nov. 29 and Dec. 15, 1999 Feb. 14, 2000 Oct. 18, 2004
Essie Cableton	Becky Williams	St. Elizabeth's	July 22, 2003
Clora T. Green	Becky Williams	St. Elizabeth's	July 22, 2003 Aug 28, 2007
Beatrice Shelby	Anita Harrison and India Fields Becky Williams	BGACDC	June 20, 2002 July 17, 2003 July 9, 2004
Chesa Owens	Cassie Currance and Tabetha Green, Becky Williams	St. Elizabeth's and at home	Aug. 3, 2002 July 22, 2003
Cora Nash	Becky Williams	St. Elizabeth's	July 23, 2003
Mae Hawkins	Becky Williams	St. Elizabeth's	July 22, 2003
Anna Huff	Anita Harrison and India Fields, Becky Williams	BGACDC and at home	June 27, 2002 July 18, 2003, Oct. 16, 2004 April 4, 2006 Aug. 7, 2007
Anita Harrison	Becky Williams	BGACDC	June 7, 2004

Appendix 3

Experiences shared by the ten women			
Name	**First Crisis**	**Second Event**	**What helped**
Gertrude Jackson	Justice – race; school segregation	Work – creation of BGACDC	Faith, family, friends, their mothers, their children, mentors, and grandmothers
Jean Davis	Justice - gender	Work – union	
Essie Cableton	Justice – work	Education – college	
Clora T. Green	Life	Life	
Beatrice Shelby	Not going to college	Justice – housing	
Chesa Owens	Justice – socio-economic, race Losing farm	Work	
Cora Nash	Death of baby	Work	
Mae Hawkins	Justice – health care	Work - nursing	
Anna Huff	Justice – race and gender School Board	Cancer	
Anita Harrison	Justice – gender Domestic violence	Justice – gender DWAG	

Appendix 4

Social justice issues and non-violent tactics employed	
Gertrude Jackson	Boycott Working group with regular meetings including neighbors Process: gather information, plan, act, reflect; repeat the process Lawsuit Community organizers – SNCC workers No direct engagement with violence of others Used strategies of other communities and locations and past experiences Learned regulations and laws – used state agency Used the media
Jean Davis	Left violent situation Union organizing Elected office
Essie Cableton	Appeal decision with lawyer
Beatrice Shelby	Protest march Petition for Governor Meeting with local agency Elected office
Chesa Owens	Investigate options and identify alternative source of funding
Mae Hawkins	Investigation Direct Action Education to obtain degree
Anna Huff	Ran for political office Door to door campaigning
Anita Harrison	Left violent situation

About the Author and Editor

Becky Williams served as co-coordinator and writer for the oral history project and worked in the two communities and with DWAG/DYAG since their
inception in 1996. Writing and working in community building for over thirty-five years, she owns Becky Williams and Associates. She partners with
community based organizations in community building and in expanding
democratic processes through the use of participatory methods including
oral histories and writing, popular education and participatory community
based research. She has been awarded writing residencies with the Wurlitzer
Foundation and Norcroft Center for Women Writers. She is a W.K. Kellogg Foundation National Fellow. She lives in Little Rock, Arkansas and rural
southern Costa Rica. She can be reached at *cypresskneepress@gmail.com*.

About the Photographer

Laurent Guerin, photojournalist has been a freelance photographer since 1993. He lived in the communities of Gould and Marvell during the summer of 2004 and photographed the women in their homes, daily routines, and in their communities. His work has appeared in publications such as Time Magazine, Chicago Tribune, The Washington Post, The New York Times, People Magazine, and The Los Angeles Times. He was contributing photographer for "The Foreign Game" by The Dayton Daily News, nominated as a finalist for Pulitzer Prize in Investigative Reporting, 2002. He resides in New Orleans, Louisiana. He can be reached at *Laurentguerin59@gmail.com*.